HUMAN RIGHTS: BACKGROUND AND ISSUES

# YOUTH IN SOLITARY CONFINEMENT

# FOCUS ON NEW YORK AND OUTSIDE PERSPECTIVES

# HUMAN RIGHTS: BACKGROUND AND ISSUES

HUMAN RIGHTS: BACKGROUND AND ISSUES

# YOUTH IN SOLITARY CONFINEMENT

## FOCUS ON NEW YORK AND OUTSIDE PERSPECTIVES

MEGHAN LLOYD
EDITOR

nova publishers
*New York*

## NOTICE TO THE READER



**Library of Congress Cataloging-in-Publication Data**

ISBN: 978-1-63483-530-5

*Published by Nova Science Publishers, Inc. † New York*

# CONTENTS

# PREFACE

On July 10, 2014, the New York Advisory Committee held a briefing on New York's use of solitary confinement (or extreme isolation, as it is sometimes termed) of youth inmates. The expert presenters included representatives from various state and city agencies and institutions in the State of New York as well as advocates and former inmates. The Committee examined the extent of the use of solitary confinement of youth in the State of New York and the City of New York, and, in particular, the disproportionate assignment of racial minorities to solitary confinement. Based on the briefing, the book discusses the history of solitary confinement within the United States; the conditions of solitary confinement in New York jails; the mental, physical and developmental effects of solitary confinement on youth in New York jails; the primary legal protections related to solitary confinement of youth inmates; and the pending legislative, judicial and executive efforts to eliminate or limit the solitary confinement of youth.

In: Youth in Solitary Confinement
Editor: Meghan Lloyd
ISBN: 978-1-63483-530-5


*Chapter 1*

# THE SOLITARY CONFINEMENT OF YOUTH IN NEW YORK: A CIVIL RIGHTS VIOLATION

***New York State Advisory Committee to the U.S. Commission on Civil Rights****

## LETTER OF TRANSMITTAL

New York Advisory Committee
to the U.S. Commission on Civil Rights

**Members of the Commission**
Martin R. Castro, *Chairperson*
Roberta Achtenberg
Gail Heriot
David Kladney
Peter N. Kirsanow
Karen Narasaki
Patricia Timmons-Goodson
Michael Yaki

Marlene Sallo, Staff Director

---

* This is an edited, reformatted and augmented version of a report issued December 2014.

The New York Advisory Committee (Committee) submits this report, "Civil Rights Implications of Solitary Confinement of Youth in New York," as part of its responsibility to advise the Commission on civil rights issues within the state. The report was adopted by the Advisory Committee by a 10 to 2 vote, with one member abstaining.

In October 2013, the Committee identified as its most pressing concern the question of whether civil rights were being violated in New York by the way in which solitary confinement was used as punishment for youth imprisoned in New York jails and prisons. The Committee held a public briefing on the issue in New York City on July 10, 2014. Presentations were made to the Committee by 17 persons on six panels, representing various state and city agencies and institutions in the State of New York as well as advocates and former inmates. The Committee examined the extent of the use of solitary confinement of youth in the State of New York and the City of New York, and, in particular, the disproportionate assignment of racial minorities to solitary confinement. The Committee also held a preparatory consultation on July 24, 2014 with experts in various states concerning the implementation of the Prison Rape Elimination Act (PREA).

This report summarizes important information from the presenters' statements, the roundtable experts, the written statements for the record, written reports and studies publicly available, and the visit of members of the Committee to Rikers Island. The report expresses concerns and observations based on the information received. The Advisory Committee trusts the Commission and the public will find the material in this report informative.

Sincerely,

Alexandra Korry, *Chairperson*
New York Advisory Committee

## EXECUTIVE SUMMARY

On July 10, 2014, the New York Advisory Committee held a briefing on New York's use of solitary confinement (or extreme isolation, as it is sometimes termed) of youth inmates. The expert presenters included representatives from various state and city agencies and institutions in the State of New York as well as advocates and former inmates. The Committee examined the extent of the use of solitary confinement of youth in the State of

New York and the City of New York, and, in particular, the disproportionate assignment of racial minorities to solitary confinement.

At the briefing, the presenters discussed (a) the history of solitary confinement within the United States, (b) the conditions of solitary confinement in New York jails, (c) the mental, physical and developmental effects of solitary confinement on youth in New York jails, (d) the primary legal protections related to solitary confinement of youth inmates and (e) the pending legislative, judicial and executive efforts to eliminate or limit the solitary confinement of youth.

In addition to the briefing, on June 25, 2014, the Committee conducted an on-site review of Rikers Island Correctional Facility (Rikers). This allowed the Committee to examine the conditions in punitive segregation units at Rikers and to speak with (i) prison officials, (ii) representatives of the New York City Department of Correction (NYC DOC) and the New York City Board of Correction (NYC BOC), and (iii) youth at Rikers who officials selected to speak with the Committee.

Lastly, the Committee held a preparatory consultation on July 24, 2014 with experts in various states concerning the implementation of the Prison Rape Elimination Act (PREA). The Committee consulted with Elissa Rumsey, Compliance Monitoring Coordinator for PREA at the U.S. Department of Justice's (DOJ) Office of Juvenile Justice and Delinquency Prevention; Teresa Abreu, Acting Executive Director for the Cook County Juvenile Temporary Juvenile Detention Center; Michael Dempsey, Executive Director of the Indiana Department of Correction's Division of Youth Services; Rick Angelozzi, Superintendent of both Columbia River Correctional Institution and South Fork Forrest Camp within the Oregon Department of Corrections; and Jason Effman, PREA Coordinator for the New York State Department of Corrections and Community Supervision (DOCCS).

Based on this record, including the documents referenced herein, the Committee offers 10 findings and makes 7 primary recommendations and 31 total recommendations—found in Section 4 of this report—and recommends that the U.S. Commission on Civil Rights call on the Department of Justice and other appropriate federal officials and agencies to use their authority to implement the Committee's recommendations.

# SECTION 1: SOLITARY CONFINEMENT IN NEW YORK

## I. Background

Despite having only five percent of the world's population,[1] the United States has almost 25 percent of its prisoners, with one in every one hundred American adults behind bars.[2] The United States has nearly as many adult prisoners (2.24 million as of October 2013) as China (1.64 million) and Russia (681,600)—the countries with the second- and third-highest prison populations—combined.[3] In fact, the United States' incarceration numbers match the rates estimated by the Committee for Human Rights in North Korea.[4] The U.S. prison population has skyrocketed in recent decades, nearly tripling between 1987 and 2007.[5] The high rates have been largely attributed to the sentencing policies accompanying the "War on Drugs," which began officially in 1982.[6] The number of Americans incarcerated for drug offenses has exploded from 41,000 in 1980 to nearly 500,000 in 2011.[7] Prisoners incarcerated on drug convictions currently make up half the federal prison population.[8]

This enormous increase in the American prison population has disproportionately affected racial minorities and youth. Specifically, as of 2012, more than 60 percent of the prison population were people of color.[9] Black men, in particular, are six times more likely than White men and two-and-a-half times more likely than Hispanic men to be incarcerated.[10] Presenters noted that it is widely known that people of color are over-represented in prisons in both adult and youth justice systems. Lisa Freeman of the Legal Aid Society indicated that "a devastating" 90 to 95 percent of the youth admitted to juvenile detention in New York City are children of color.[11]

According to the New York State Division of Criminal Justices Services, of the approximately 800 16- and 17-year-olds arrested in New York in 2010 (latest available data) who were sentenced to prison or jail time, two-thirds were Black, 26 percent were Latino, and 5 percent were White.[12] Racial disparities in incarceration have also been attributed, in part, to disproportionate sentencing of White men and Black men for similar crimes. Indeed, an analysis by the U.S. Sentencing Commission found that sentences for Black men were nearly 20 percent longer than those for White men convicted of similar crimes and that this gap has widened since the Supreme Court restored judicial discretion in federal sentencing in 2005.[13]

The number of youth housed in adult jails has also drastically increased in recent years. In fact, the number of youth in adult jails more than tripled between 1983 and 1998.[14] As of 2010, there were an estimated 139,000 children under the age of 18 in adult jails and prisons.[15]

### *A. History of Solitary Confinement in the United States*

The earliest use of solitary confinement in the United States can be traced backed to Walnut-Street Penitentiary in Philadelphia, Pennsylvania in 1787 where it was employed as a rehabilitative tool.[16] The theory behind its use was that if a prisoner were to be left alone with only his conscience and a Bible, he would have time to reflect on his bad deeds, come to see the nature of his crimes and voluntarily reform into a law-abiding citizen.[17] As early as 1890, however, the U.S. Supreme Court noted that solitary confinement did not have a rehabilitative quality. In *In re Medley*, the Supreme Court reported that:

> A considerable number of the prisoners fell, after even a short confinement, into a semi-fatuous condition, from which it was next to impossible to arouse them, and others became violently insane; others still, committed suicide; while those who stood the ordeal better were not generally reformed, and in most cases did not recover sufficient mental activity to be of any subsequent service to the community.[18]

The consensus that solitary confinement was inhumane and ineffective led to its general abandonment in the United States for more than a century.[19] However, in the mid-1900s, solitary confinement returned as a prison management tool.[20] By 1991, Human Rights Watch reported that 36 states, including New York, had built or repurposed existing facilities devoted to the extreme isolation of prisoners for 23 hours per day.[21]

### *B. Use of Solitary Confinement in the United States Today*

Consistent with the high rates of incarceration nationwide, the Bureau of Justice Statistics estimates that the United States holds over 80,000 people in segregation units[22]—more than any other democratic country.[23] According to experts, this number represents only a fraction of the state and federal prisoners who spend time in "high-security control units" over the course of a year and does not include everyone incarcerated in supermax prisons or local jails.[24] Further, the use of segregated housing has outpaced the growth of the prison population.[25]

The statistics with respect to the use of solitary confinement and other isolation practices on youth inmates are similarly concerning. While there is no comprehensive national data on the solitary confinement of children in the United States, the most recent estimate from the Bureau of Justice Statistics data suggests that about 35,000 youth between ages 10 and 20 were held in isolation in juvenile facilities (*i.e.*, not including inmates under 21 in adult facilities).[26] More than half of those children were held for more than 24 hours in some form of solitary confinement.[27]

According to Ian M. Kysel, Adjunct Professor of Law and Dash/Muse Fellow at the Georgetown Law Human Rights Institute, based on the data reflected in a 2012 report he authored on the use of solitary confinement on youth in the United States, each year, nearly 100,000 children are held in jails and prisons where solitary confinement is used as a prison management tool.[28] The data reflects that jail and prison officials use the same techniques — including solitary confinement — to manage children as they do for adults.[29] For example, some large state jail and prison systems have reported that over 10 percent of children in their facilities are subjected to solitary confinement, and some smaller facilities have reported that 100 percent of the children imprisoned there are held in isolation.[30] Professor Kysel wrote that, in general, the purpose for using solitary confinement for youth is (a) to punish them when they break the rules, (b) to manage them — either to protect them from adults or one another, or because officials do not know how else to handle them or (c) to medically treat them after a suicide threat or attempt.[31]

As Professor Kysel noted, the current use of solitary confinement in the United States flies in the face of every set of national standards governing age and developmentally appropriate practices to manage children in rehabilitative or correctional settings, as these national standards strictly limit all forms of isolation.[32] The DOJ Standards for the Administration of Juvenile Justice, for example, recommends that youth be held in isolation for no longer than 24 hours.[33] And the American Academy of Child and Adolescent Psychiatry (AACAP) recommends a complete ban on solitary confinement for youth.[34]

## II. Solitary Confinement in New York

### *A. Overview of New York Prison System*

#### 1. New York State Department of Corrections and Community Supervision

New York State Department of Corrections and Community Supervision (DOCCS) holds approximately 54,000 inmates in 54 different correctional facilities and supervises 36,000 parolees.[35] Consistent with the national movement towards the use of solitary confinement, over the past two decades,

New York State has spent hundreds of millions of dollars to build and operate a large scale network of extreme isolation cells called "Special Housing Units" or "SHUs."[36] Between 1998 and 2000, New York State constructed 10 additional facilities devoted to extreme isolation.[37] The construction of these facilities coincided with the rise of New York State's prison population during the 1980s and 1990s. In 1983, New York State's prison population was 30,951, rising to 54,895 in 1990 and a high of 71,466 in 1999.[38]

At any given time, nearly 4,500 inmates in New York are subjected to isolated confinement.[39] New York State currently has two exclusive SHU facilities — Southport (789 beds) and Upstate (1,040 beds) — as well as eight designated SHU buildings on the premises of medium-security prisons, each of which has 200 SHU beds.[40] There are 29 additional facilities in New York State that have SHU beds separated from the general prison population.[41] In addition to SHUs, some New York State facilities subjected inmates to extreme isolation by sentencing them to a "keeplock," imposed as punishment for less serious disciplinary infractions.[42] According to a New York Civil Liberties Union (NYCLU) report, keeplock inmates are subjected to 23-hour lockdown either in their own cells within the prison population or are transferred to a designated block of keeplock cells in the same facility.[43] About 10 percent of inmates sentenced to keeplock are actually housed in a SHU cell with the same restrictions as those sentenced directly to SHUs.[44]

Unfortunately, according to the DOCCS Commissioner Anthony J. Annucci, because these under-resourced SHUs were constructed a certain way, it will be very expensive to change them to address the issues that are noted later in this report.[45]

### 2. New York City Department of Correction

The New York City Department of Correction (NYC DOC) handles over 100,000 admissions per year and manages approximately 14,000 inmates at any given time.[46] The vast majority of inmates are held in 10 facilities at the Rikers Island Correctional Facility (Rikers).[47] The majority of inmates at Rikers are pre-trial detainees.[48] Additional facilities are located in Brooklyn, Manhattan, Queens and a floating jail barge in the Bronx.[49] Of the 14 NYC DOC facilities, six were built between 1983 and 1991,[50] coinciding with the explosive increase in inmates statewide. Medical services within the NYC DOC are the responsibility of the New York City Department of Health and Mental Health (DOHMH).[51] The NYC Board of Correction (NYC BOC) is charged with monitoring conditions in the City's jails, investigating serious incidents, evaluating the performance of the NYC DOC, reviewing inmate and employee grievances, and making recommendations in critical areas of correctional planning."[52] In that capacity, the NYC BOC, an independent oversight and regulatory body, promulgates the rules and regulations that govern the New York City jails and ensures compliance with those rules and regulations.[53]

Most adolescent male inmates at Rikers are housed at the Robert N. Davoren Complex (RNDC).[54] Within the RNDC, 18-year-old inmates are now housed in separate units so they no longer interact with 16- and 17-year-old inmates.[55] Once sentenced, inmates are placed in the Eric M. Taylor Center (EMTC) which houses inmates sentenced to one year or less.[56] Inmates placed in punitive segregation after being found guilty of an infraction or who are awaiting a hearing on an infraction are placed in the Central Punitive Segregation Unit (CPSU) at the Otis Bantum Correctional Center (OBCC).[57] The CPSU has capacity for up to 50 adolescent inmates who are housed in a block of punitive segregation cells.[58] Adolescents can also be held in strict solitary confinement with 23 hours of lockdown in the RNDC, as well as a modified solitary for those who are mentally ill in the RNDC's Restrictive Housing Unit (RHU) at RNDC, which provides some clinical interventions.[59] Until its closure in late 2013, up to 50 mentally ill adolescent inmates were housed in the Mental Health Assessment Unit for Infracted Inmates (MHAUII).[60] Since the Committee briefing in July, 2014, most 18-year-old inmates have been transferred to the George Motchan Detention Center and the George R. Vierno Center and serve their solitary confinement time in the OBCC.

### 3. Due Process in the Imposition of Solitary Confinement

DOCCS regulations list more than 100 rules that inmates must obey.[61] According to Karen Murtagh, the Executive Director of Prisoners' Legal Services (PLS), there are "too many rules that are easy to violate." [62] Each rule has a predetermined range of "tier ratings" that the review officer will assign depending on the severity of the infraction: (a) tier I to tier II, (b) tier II to tier III, or (c) tier I to tier III.[63] An inmate convicted of a tier II or tier III infraction may ultimately receive a punishment of extreme isolation after a formal disciplinary hearing.[64] At the hearing— at which the inmate is not afforded legal counsel—the inmate has an opportunity to respond to the charges and evidence, call witnesses, as well as submit evidence and written statements, but is not allowed to cross-examine witnesses.[65] The standard of proof required to put a person in punitive segregation is "substantial evidence," which simply means that the evidence required is more than 50-50.[66] From

2007 to 2011, of the over 105,500 hearings involving tier III infractions, nearly 95 percent resulted in a conviction[67] and approximately 68 percent of convictions resulted in a sentence to the SHU.[68] Further, once an inmate, regardless of age, is sent to solitary confinement, New York State law sets no limit as to the amount of time the inmate may spend there.[69] As a result, disciplinary segregation sentences can last anywhere from a few weeks to several years.

According to Barbara Hamilton, Staff Attorney at The Legal Aid Society Criminal Defense Practice Special Litigation Unit, the NYC DOC appeal process is different from the DOCCS system in that inmates in NYC DOC custody are automatically assigned an attorney if they appeal the determination. The attorney reviews the administrative determination that resulted in solitary confinement time.[70] The hearings are presided over by an adjudication captain, who is a NYC DOC employee and typically a former correction officer.[71] Judge Hamill highlighted the problems that exist with the disciplinary hearing process:

> What I have learned from reviewing that policy and by speaking to some of the inmates and speaking to many of the captains that do the hearings, is that, in general, they are not provided any type of right to counsel, that there is no—and we are still investigating this—that there is no sworn[] evidence that's presented against the inmates. There are statements that are collected and then that is read into the record by the hearing captain and relied upon. It's not notarized or sworn to under penalty of perjury, and the investigating officers and the like are not called in to testify. The inmates are then asked to respond to the allegations; they are given an opportunity to bring forth witnesses if the witnesses are actually present in that facility, and there is no real meaningful consideration about the mental health aspect.[72]

John Perez, a Reentry Mental Health Advocate at the Urban Justice Center who spent 13 years in a New York prison—including three years in a SHU double bunk and one year in isolated confinement—told the Committee that correctional officers tend to retaliate against those who express discontent with how punishments are administered.[73] Mr. Perez also noted that in hearings following the receipt of a "ticket" for an infraction, the officers often intimidate inmates to force them to accept punishments for acts they had not committed.[74] Mr. Perez explained, "[f]or the most part you tend to comply, you tend to try to pick the lesser of the two evils, you try to pick the lesser of the consequences."[75] Mr. Perez cited the example of an officer who said to an inmate:

> "Look, if you fight this I am going to slay you." In other words, I am going to give you the maximum amount of time I can give you in the box and good luck later with trying to appeal. As a result a lot of people plea bargain and say, "Look I did it," you know, even if you didn't do it and hope for a minimum amount of time.[76]

However, as Ms. Hamilton told the Committee, the assumption is incorrect that admitting to the original offense will lead to a lenient punishment.[77]

### 4. Grounds for Use of Solitary Confinement

A commonly cited rationale for the widespread use of solitary confinement is the dangerousness of the offending inmate.[78] Indeed, DOCCS Commissioner Annucci told the Committee that in order to ensure the safety of the inmates—one of his main responsibilities as Commissioner of DOCCS—there is a need to segregate some individuals from others.[79]

Inmates, however, are often placed in isolation for non-violent misbehavior. In fact, from 2007 to 2011, only 16 percent of SHU sentences were for infractions related to violent misbehavior such as assault.[80] Similarly, during the same time period, 23 percent of all tier III disciplinary proceedings resulting in SHU sentences were for drug-related infractions.[81] Although tier III is supposed to define only the most serious infractions, the range of offenses that qualify as tier III infractions encompass even minor forms of insubordination, such as talking back to a corrections officer, refusing a direct order, or not returning a food tray. These broad categories of offenses could include mere sluggishness in responding to a command or an impulsive complaint or query about an order—normal behavior for adolescents with less self-discipline than an adult. Because NYC DOC rules do not provide for any review of the proportionality of sentences, impulsive and non-threatening exclamations can land an adolescent inmate in solitary confinement.

There seems to be recognition from DOCCS leadership that the discretion of corrections staff to impose solitary confinement for minor infractions is not adequately circumscribed by the language of DOCCS' rules. DOCCS Commissioner Annucci noted that "refusal to obey a direct order can be very minor" and that "the word assault . . . can encompass everything under the sun."[82] Acknowledging that DOCCS needs "to do some soul searching and say we have to separate someone who's dangerous as opposed to someone who is joking around," DOCCS Commissioner Annucci emphasized the role of personnel training to enable staff to draw the necessary distinctions. DOCCS is currently drafting new guidelines to circumscribe discretion over the use of solitary confinement as part of the settlement of *Peoples* v. *Fischer*.[83] By contrast, NYC DOC has not made any apparent effort to circumscribe the discretion to impose solitary confinement with specific and enforceable proportionality standards.

Sentence lengths are also exacerbated by what is known as "owed time." New York City Council Member Daniel Dromm told the Committee about a man he had watched grow up and who was sentenced to 150 days of punitive segregation for the possession of cigarettes in prison despite being in severe need of mental health and substance abuse assistance.[84] This inmate only served 120 days of his solitary sentence before he was sent upstate and eventually released.[85] However, when he returned to Rikers after reoffending, he was immediately placed back into solitary confinement to complete the 30 days he had left under the original sentence.[86] Judge Bryanne Hamill, a retired New York City Family Court judge and Chair of the NYC BOC, Adolescent and Young Adult Rulemaking Committee, indicated that eliminating owed time was an important issue related to solitary confinement that the NYC BOC was reviewing.[87]

Ms. Hamilton indicated that disobeying staff orders is one of the top infractions that leads to solitary confinement.[88] Five Mualimm-Ak, a former inmate and Founder and Executive Director of the Incarcerated Nation Campaign who served 12 years in prison at Rikers and upstate facilities (five of them in solitary confinement), told the Committee that in his experience as an inmate at Rikers and upstate facilities, youth inmates could be sent to solitary confinement "for talking back, for looking the wrong way, for literally forgetting to pick up their fork in a mess hall."[89] And as Angela Browne from the Vera Institute noted, ". . . you can get a year [in solitary] for something that I think to many people would sound inappropriate, violations such as talking out of place, failing to go to work or school, [or] refusing to change cells."[90]

Ms. Hamilton also noted that fighting is the second most common infraction — a fact that is not surprising because exposure to isolation increases an inmate's psychosis and violent behavior.[91] Mr. Mualimm-Ak said that when an incident broke out at Rikers everyone involved would be sent to solitary confinement without investigation and that oftentimes an inmate could spend a week in solitary confinement before knowing whether he would be kept there.[92]

Yet, the use of punitive segregation to deal with problematic behavior does not result in a more controlled jail environment.[93] Beth Powers of the New York Children's Defense Fund told the Committee that, as the number of isolation beds at Rikers increased 61 percent from 2007 to 2013, "use of force" incidents actually tripled despite a reduced inmate population over that period.[94] Council Member Dromm, noting the liberal use of solitary confinement as a management tool, said that the "imposition of severe isolation for infractions unrelated to safety concerns seems to serve no purpose other than to brutalize prisoners."[95]

Despite its documented lack of effectiveness, trends indicate an increased reliance on the use of punitive segregation. Between 2004 and 2013, the NYC DOC prison population being held in isolated confinement increased from 2.7 percent to 7.5 percent.[96] Further, between 2007 and 2013, the number of NYC DOC punitive segregation beds increased from 614 to 998.[97] During roughly that same time period, the total reported number of self-mutilation incidents and suicide attempts increased from 480 to 850 for all inmates.[98]

## *B. Youth in the New York Prison System*

### 1. Age of Criminal Responsibility in New York

New York is one of only two states that treat 16- and 17-year-olds automatically as adults,[99] and the age of criminal responsibility in New York State can, for certain especially heinous offenses, begin as low as 13 even though these children cannot legally be bound by a contract, get married without parental consent, vote, or sit on juries in New York State.[100] Thus, 16- and 17-year-olds who are arrested are transported from the police precinct directly to adult criminal court for arraignment.[101] If the 16- or 17-year-old is not released on recognizance or bail, then the juvenile is sent to a DOCCS or NYC DOC facility.[102] Although it is possible for some 16- and 17-yearolds to be granted a "Youthful Offender" status, this status does not prevent them from being treated as adults. Rather, Youthful Offender status ensures that the conviction will not result in a criminal record, and offers a more lenient sentencing structure. The finding of "Youthful Offender" status is not made until the sentencing hearing.[103] Therefore, a 16- or 17-year-old who is arrested in New York City and cannot post bail could end up spending months in an adult jail such as Rikers before any finding is made as to whether that defendant is guilty. For example, Ms. Freeman described her experience with a 16-year-old youth who, had been in New York City Administration for Children Services (ACS) custody when he was accused of assaulting another youth. Although ACS does not rely on the use of isolation to manage youth, once this youth was transferred to Rikers — since he was 16 at the time of the incident — he was repeatedly subjected to solitary confinement for over eight months. Ultimately, the case was dismissed and he was returned to ACS custody.[104] Youth defendants are subject to New York State's mandatory sentencing guidelines, leaving judges with limited discretion when it comes to sentencing a youth defendant.[105]

Judge Michael Corriero, former New York State Judge and current Executive Director and Founder of the New York Center for Juvenile Justice, called "the idea that if you steal a piece of bread from a grocery store at 16 and you can't make bail that you will go to a place like Rikers Island" an "abomination," noting that these youth inmates "will be subject to the punitive segregation standards that the officials at Rikers Island use to tame the adult population."[106] Judge Corriero noted that New York is "an outlier in the way it treats adolescents who get into trouble by treating them as adults" and further opined that "it is because of this systemic lens by which we view children as adults that they are now exposed to punitive segregation techniques that have always been apparently used to tame adults."[107] Judge Corriero argued that there is "absolutely no moral justification for punitive segregation" of children, and that this is especially egregious "in the state, which has in its harbor the Statue of Liberty, that has always welcomed the poor and powerless."[108]

## 2. Statistical Overview of the Youth in New York Prisons

As of January 2012, DOCCS had 181 juveniles in its custody.[109] The NYC DOC currently manages 303 adolescent inmates,[110] and averaged 489 inmates aged 16 through 18 during the 2014 fiscal year.[111] NYC DOC Commissioner Joseph Ponte told the Committee that adolescent inmates represent a significant management challenge to the NYC DOC. For example, although they account for only 2.5 percent of the average daily population, adolescents are involved in 17 percent of all violent incidents, and the average length of stay of an adolescent inmate is nearly three weeks longer (74 days) than the average length of stay for adult inmates (54 days).[112] Mr. Ponte added that this is "due in large measure" to the fact that 77 percent of adolescent inmates are charged with a violent felony as compared with only 38 percent of adult inmates.[113]

Dr. Homer D. Venters, Assistant Commissioner DOHMH, Bureau of Correctional Health Services, told the Committee that despite their relatively small share of the overall population, adolescents are overrepresented in other vulnerable cohorts, including those who receive mental health services, those who are treated for injuries, and those in solitary confinement.[114]

## C. Solitary Confinement of Youth in New York

Data about the solitary confinement of children in New York State are not systematically or publicly reported and the available data do not account for the use of solitary confinement by county jail systems in New York State other than New York City.[115] Therefore, the Committee was not able to obtain any reliable information on the number of youth held in solitary confinement in state, county or local facilities in New York State. However, the statistics that have been reported reveal that, as of July 23, 2013, 140 adolescent inmates were in some form of solitary confinement in the New York State prison system.[116] In January 2012, over 400 inmates in extreme isolation in New York State were under the age of 20, and 83 of these were teenagers between the ages of 16 and 18.[117]

Within the NYC DOC, New York City officials have reported that 14.4 percent of adolescents between the ages of 16 and 18 at Rikers spend at least some time in punitive segregation.[118] According to Commissioner Ponte, approximately 18 percent of adolescents under the custody of the NYC DOC are in punitive segregation at any time.[119] In the summer of 2013, between 25 and 28 percent of adolescent boys reportedly spent some time in solitary confinement.[120] The average length of stay in solitary confinement reported by NYC DOC was 43.1 days;[121] however, as Judge Corriero noted, any inmate in the custody of the NYC DOC repeatedly can receive punitive segregation for periods not exceeding 90 days for each individual disciplinary charge.[122] Scott Paltrowitz of the Correctional Association of New York, a nonprofit group with a legislative mandate to investigate prisons and advocate for improved conditions,[123] explained that inmates "get ticket after ticket after ticket" when in the SITU because any subsequent infraction leads to added time:

> So people might serve . . . 90 days on the first ticket and then you refuse to give a food tray back or you talk back to an officer or you stick your arm out of the slot in the door and you get another ticket for sixty days, you get another ticket for three months, and you get another ticket for six months and all of that time adds up to three years, five years, ten years[,] twenty years in solitary.[124]

With respect to Rikers in particular, the U.S. Department of Justice (DOJ) concluded in an August 4, 2014 letter sent to New York City Mayor Bill de Blasio, NYC DOC Commissioner Joseph Ponte, and New York Corporation

Counsel Zachary Carter (DOJ Letter) that it was "clear that adolescents" — defined as male inmates between the ages of 16 and 18 — "at Rikers receive infractions at an extraordinarily high rate and spend an exorbitant amount of time in punitive segregation."[125] Specifically, in only a 21-month span, 3,158 adolescent inmates at Rikers received a total of 143,823 sentence days.[126] The DOJ also found that sentences were excessively long. For example, of the 57 inmates in the RNDC CPSU on February 1, 2013, 36 were sentenced to 60 days or more, including 22 inmates with sentences between 90 and 188 days and two with sentences exceeding 200 days.[127] During the Committee's June 25, 2014 visit to Rikers, the Committee walked past doors of two under 18-year-old inmates with solitary sentences of 150 and 138 days, respectively.

The subject of excessive aggregate solitary confinement sentences is an issue within DOCCS's facilities as well. Ms. Murtagh provided an example of a 17-year-old client named Raymond who currently has a 39-month solitary confinement sentence as a result of 23 hearings over a 9- month period.[128] Currently, there is no administrative process within DOCCS for directly challenging excessive aggregate penalties. Therefore, the only alternative is to appeal each hearing individually.[129]

The high rates of youth subjected to solitary confinement may be due, in part, to their lack of understanding of the punishment process. Ms. Hamilton told the Committee that there are two main factors at Rikers preventing youth from obtaining optimum outcomes at disciplinary hearings. First, there is the institutional assumption that all inmates are guilty.[130] This is due, in part, to the fact that many adjudicators are former correction officers.[131] Second, many youth inmates do not understand what is going on at the hearing and believe—incorrectly—that admitting to the initial charge will absolve a solitary confinement sentence.[132] The procedural misunderstanding also is the reason why many inmates do not appeal their solitary confinement sentences.[133]

Another contributing factor to the high rates of solitary confinement sentences is the culture of violence that persists among both inmates and correction officers. Youth inmates, in particular, have described that they often feel a need to fight in prison. For example, Jennifer Parish, director of Criminal Justice Advocacy at the Urban Justice Center's Mental Health Project, told the Committee that youth inmates frequently speak with her about the violence in prison and "of fighting [which] lands them in the box, about how it's necessary [to fight] when you're in jail and that when they do it, it results in them being in the box."[134] Ms. Freeman reiterated this point, explaining that one inmate told her that "[t]he way you have to operate to be safe in Rikers [is] you have to hit somebody before they are expecting it so that everyone knows to be afraid of you[.] [O]therwise essentially you're going to be picked on."[135] The DOJ reported that in 2013 there were 845 inmate-on-inmate fights involving adolescents at the RNDC and EMTC facilities at Rikers, but also that there is good reason to suspect that fights are even more prevalent than the data reflects.[136]

In addition to inmate-on-inmate fights, adolescent inmates are subjected to excessive force at the hands of correction officers. For example, the DOJ found that at Rikers, "DOC staff routinely use force unnecessarily as a means to control the adolescent population and punish disobedient or disrespectful inmates in clear violation of DOC policy. Even when some level of force is necessary, the force used is often disproportionate to the risk posed by the inmate, frequently resulting in serious injuries to inmates and staff."[137] In 2013 alone, there were 565 reported staff use of force incidents involving adolescents in RNDC and EMTC.[138] These numbers are particularly alarming considering the average daily adolescent population was only 682 over that same period.[139] As of October 2012, 43.7 percent of the adolescent males in custody had been subjected to use of force by Rikers staff.[140]

Mr. Paltrowitz also described the high levels of physical and verbal abuse by correction officers against young inmates in the DOCCS system. He noted that during his visit to Greene Correctional Facility (Greene), he found high levels of physical and verbal abuse and intimidation even when compared with notoriously violent facilities such as the Attica Correctional Facility or the Clinton Correctional Facility.[141] According to Mr. Paltrowitz, 86 percent of the people who entered the DOCCS system at the age of 16 or 17 reported being in a physical confrontation with staff while at Greene, compared to a 26 percent average for all other facilities visited by the organization.[142] Moreover, 97 percent of the inmates his organization surveyed indicated that young inmates between 16 and 17 years of age are more likely to be abused by staff than the rest of the inmates.[143] Mr. Mualimm-Ak described seeing correction officers using chains on adolescent inmates to beat, injure, mentally harass, and physically abuse them.[144]

Two final considerations regarding New York's use of solitary confinement concern the racial disparity of inmates subjected to isolation and the use of solitary confinement on mentally ill inmates. With respect to percentages by race, consistent with the overall national incarceration trends, youth of color in New York are overrepresented in New York prisons.[145] Black and Hispanic youth represent 70 percent of 16- and 17-year-olds arrested in New York State, but are 80 percent of youth sentenced to incarceration in New York State.[146] This disproportionality is even more extreme in New York City, with youth of color representing 88 percent of those arrested and 94 percent of the arrests resulting in incarceration.[147] As noted by Judge Corriero, many of these youth come from New York's poorest and most underserved communities.[148]

The disparate treatment continues once inmates of color are sent to prison. Black inmates, in particular, make up 49.5 percent of the general prison population, but 59 percent of the extreme isolation population.[149] These numbers are staggering considering that only 17.6 percent of New York State's population is Black.[150]

Finally, regarding mentally ill inmates, New York State and New York City facilities restrict use of solitary confinement on mentally ill youth inmates. Within DOCCS facilities, a 2011 law (the SHU Exclusion Law) requires that inmates with serious mental illness be diverted from extreme isolation to units jointly operated by DOCCS and the New York State Office of Mental Health (OMH), whose purpose is therapeutic and not disciplinary.[151] Within New York City, youth inmates who have been determined to be mentally ill are placed in a second type of solitary confinement—an RHU that provides individual behavioral and group therapy.[152] The RHU follows a system with incentives for good behavior through a "three-tiered reward system" in which the inmates are rewarded with increasing non-isolation time as they engage in active therapy sessions and demonstrate a good behavior goal.[153] These mentally ill youth inmates are always handcuffed and shackled, even during group therapy sessions.[154] Non-violent inmates with non-violent Grade II or III infractions who complete the program can have their segregation time reduced by 50 percent.[155] According to the DOJ report, although the NYC DOC touts the RHU program as an accomplishment, as of October 1, 2013, only 29 of the hundreds of adolescents placed in the RHU program had received a reduction in their segregation time.[156]

### 1. Conditions of Confinement

Solitary confinement of youth is characterized by extreme isolation both in New York State and New York City facilities. By design, the New York State SHU facilities prevent inmates from social interaction. Inmates live in a "space capsule" cell barely larger than a king-sized bed with minimal human contact.[157] Inmates are isolated for 23 hours per day.[158] According to DOCCS Commissioner Annucci, however, as a result of recent changes, 16- and 17-year-old inmates "will be afforded a maximum of five hours per day . . . out of cell time," which includes four hours of therapeutic treatment and one hour of recreational time.[159]

Not only are inmates in solitary confinement isolated from the other inmates, but they also suffer from a deeper and more profound isolation from the outside world.[160] As Professor Kysel explained:

> Sometimes children can communicate with each other – yelling to other children, voices distorted, reverberating against concrete and metal. In some facilities, children get a book, or maybe just a Bible, or perhaps study materials slipped under their door. But in solitary confinement, few contours distinguish one hour, day or week from the next.[161]

In contrast to in-cell confinement, SHU cells are typically designed to be more desensitizing and more dehumanizing.[162] Food, for example, is provided through a slot in the door.[163] Inmates in the SHU also cannot make any phone calls, and family visits are complicated and discouraged. Inmates are restrained by handcuffs secured to a waist chain and are separated from their loved ones by a physical barrier.[164] They are not allowed to attend school; instead, schoolwork is provided on worksheets and through phone calls.[165] The SHU facilities lack any educational, vocational, or rehabilitative programs of any kind.[166] As a result, inmates usually spend their time pacing, sleeping, reading, and writing.[167] Through good behavior, inmates may also earn a pair of headphones set to a pre-selected radio station.[168]

Moreover, DOCCS regulations permit "deprivation orders" that strip inmates in the SHU of any "specific item, privilege, or service when it is determined that a threat to the safety or security of staff, inmates, or State property exists."[169] The deprivation can include denial of showers, recreation, cell-cleaning supplies, haircuts, clothing, bedding, towels, and even food.[170] With respect to food deprivation in particular, SHU inmates who commit certain disciplinary infractions may be punished with a "restricted diet,"[171] also known as "the loaf" or the "loaf diet."[172] The loaf is a small, "gross tasting" loaf made with ground up carrots, whole wheat flour and salt.[173] Usually imposed on inmates for misbehavior, this loaf is served three times a day with a half a cup of cold cabbage and a glass of water. This diet, which requires the authorization of a doctor, as well as a blood pressure test every day during the diet, can last for seven days followed by a three-day break.[174]

In certain cases, an inmate in SHU wakes up with another inmate in the same cell. Cellmates must then share space of approximately 100 square feet — about the size of a parking spot — that includes a toilet, open shower stall, writing platform and bunk beds.[175] The resulting lack of privacy often creates tension, especially while showering or using the toilet. No curtain or barrier separates the shower or the toilet from the rest of the cell. Consequently, inmates are forced to expose themselves to their cellmates.[176]

New York City confinement conditions are comparable to the solitary confinement conditions in New York State facilities. Young inmates sentenced to punitive solitary confinement at Rikers Island — the CPSU, also called the "Bing" or the "Box"[177] — are taken to a six-by-eight-foot single cell for 23 to 24 hours a day.[178] They are given the right to have one hour of recreation per day and access to a daily shower.[179] Meals are taken alone in the inmate's cell and are provided through slots on the door of the segregation units.[180]

Even when an inmate is granted time out of solitary confinement for recreation, the time is spent in individual chain-link cages.[181] Because inmates remain shackled and are searched beforehand, very few inmates take advantage of the time.[182] In July 2014, the NYC BOC released a staff report entitled "Barriers to Recreation at Rikers Island's Central Punitive Segregation Unit (CPSU)," which outlined why "recreation is an infrequent event within the CPSU rather than part of an inmate's daily routine."[183] Specifically, the study revealed that 87.8 percent of the survey respondents indicated that they did not participate in recreation on any of the four consecutive days that were the subject of the survey.[184] The study also reported that four out of every five inmates were not even afforded the opportunity to sign up for recreation.[185] The main reason cited for the lack of participation is that announcements were inaudible or made when inmates were asleep.[186]

A number of other factors — besides the lack of opportunity to sign up — have been cited for these low numbers, including (a) the lack of officers supervising recreation posts and activities, (b) the lack of indoor recreation areas for use during inclement weather, (c) the lack of equipment or structures in the outdoor cages to facilitate exercise, (d) depression, and (e) the reluctance to be searched and shackled just to be taken to an outdoor cage.[187]

Youth inmates also are often denied adequate mental healthcare while in punitive segregation. *Three Adolescents with Mental Illness in Punitive Segregation at Rikers Island* — a report prepared by and for the NYC BOC — details the poor quality of mental health treatment for three young people with mental illness while held in isolated confinement settings in the New York City jails.[188] The report found that these adolescents were sentenced to isolated confinement terms lasting up to 200 days and suffered significant maltreatment.[189] For example, the youth were often denied access to mental healthcare providers.[190] Even when group therapy was provided in the mental health wing, inmates were shackled.[191]

And, during individual therapy, inmates were forced to have their sessions through their cell doors (*i.e.*, within earshot of staff and other inmates).[192] Mr. Dromm told the Committee that during a visit to Rikers he saw an inmate with his wrist chained to a pipe in front of him while attending a therapy session, and questioned how effective a therapy session could be under those dehumanizing conditions.[193] Mr. Dromm reflected about the perverse culture of neglect for those in isolation around both medical and mental health services and referenced the NYCLU report, which found that isolation psychologically harms both inmates and correction officers.[194] The Committee also witnessed a group of inmates preparing for group therapy, chained to their benches several feet from one another.

In contrast to the conditions noted above, New York City Administration for Children's Services (ACS) and New York State Office of Children and Family Services (OCFS) facilities employ a room confinement model where the child is placed in room confinement only if he or she is an imminent danger to himself/herself or others.[195] Confinement cannot last more than 24 hours except with high-level approval from the agency.[196] While there can be issues with the implementation of these policies as well, this approach is preferred by many experts in this field.[197]

### 2. Testimonial from 16-Year-old Inmate at Rikers

Accompanying the testimonials discussed above — including the personal experiences in solitary confinement of presenters Mr. Mualimm-Ak and Mr. Perez — the Committee heard from Jennifer Parish, Director of Criminal Justice Advocacy at the Urban Justice Center's Mental Health Project, about a 16-year-old client who was incarcerated at Rikers. Ms. Parish explained that the boy was sent to isolation for fighting with other inmates who tried to take his food and to make him buy them things with the commissary dollars his family sent him.[198]

After spending between 22 and 24 hours in isolation per day, the boy became depressed and suicidal. Although he told the correction officers he was thinking about suicide, he said they did not care.[199] He explained that for the first week in solitary confinement he was not allowed to shower, go outside, call his parents, or do schoolwork.[200] Ms. Parish noted that the boy did not receive a proper diet while in isolation and therefore became malnourished, weighing only 100 pounds at 5 feet 4 inches tall.[201]

Ms. Parish read at the July 10 briefing in the boy's own words:

It's about to get really hot, but right now the nights are so cold. I sleep in my uniform wrapped in the blanket we get and I am still so cold, but it's better than burning up when summer hits. I sleep with my cell light on because I don't want the roaches and mice to come. . . .

I am underweight, I should be getting extra starch, milk and cereal and fruit. I haven't been getting these in the box, sometimes they don't feed me at all. If someone getting his food in front of me decides to block his slot by sticking his arm out the hole in his door and refusing to put it back inside when that happens the CO's just stop feeding everyone and we all go hungry. I have been prescribed Remeron the psychiatric medication to help me sleep, but often the same thing happens, someone blocks the slot and no one gets their medicine. There is also a limit on hygiene products. I am not allowed to shave. I do get a toothbrush and toothpaste but once I run out, the CO's take a while to replace it. While in the box I have seen officers beat up an inmate with sticks. I have also seen them tell inmates to beat up somebody or they'll bribe someone with a pen or [do-]rag. Officers have told me "you're a black bitch" that is why you're in jail.

The only way to complain about this kind of treatment is to call 311, but we hardly ever get the phone. Anyway the CO's mark that process. At the end of the day I will go home and you're in jail they say. Some inmates cry all day, crying doesn't help, you still have to do your days. I started talking to myself out loud. I will talk about what I am going to do when I go home. Sometimes I think that people are calling me, but no one is. My court date is tomorrow I hope I get to go home with my mom and grandmother soon.[202]

Ms. Parish explained that the conditions the boy described were not unique and that she has heard the same accounts many times after interviewing people.[203] Inmates describe to her their feelings of being isolated, of medication denials, of racial slurs, of religious discrimination, and of lack of nutritious food.[204]

### 3. Governmental and Legal Efforts at Reform

As awareness of this issue has grown, the process of reforming the use of solitary confinement in New York has begun. The recent policy changes and ongoing efforts include the following, which are described in greater detail in Section 3 and in other portions of this report:

- In late 2013, the NYC DOC implemented new sentencing guidelines as a response to the increased scrutiny of its disciplinary system.[205] In general, the sentencing guidelines aim to reduce the amount of time that inmates spend in solitary confinement.[206] Under the new guidelines, sentences for multiple nonviolent infractions are supposed to run concurrently, as opposed to consecutively.[207] Furthermore, previously-accumulated segregation time will be expunged after a certain period and will not carry over to any potential re-incarceration.[208] Finally, inmates sentenced to punitive incarceration may earn a conditional discharge after completing 66 percent of their sentence if they break no rules while isolated.[209] The DOJ Letter noted that "although these reforms are a positive step, it is too early to assess their impact."[210]

- For seriously mentally ill inmates, solitary confinement was eliminated in 2013.[211] Seriously mentally ill children are now taken to Clinical Alternatives to Punitive Segregation (CAPS) units.[212] To date, three CAPS units have opened: two for male inmates and one for female inmates.[213] According to Dr. Venters, the results of these units are promising, with CAPS units experiencing rates of violence and self-harm that are less than half of the rates of units where patients had been previously housed.[214] For example, CAPS units report about 40 acts of self-harm per 1,000 patients, compared to 260 acts of self-harm per 1,000 patients in RHUs.[215]
- In order to address the violence issue and to conform to federal law, Rikers decided—as did New York State prisons — to separate 18-year-olds from 16- and 17-year-olds.[216] This separation has been beneficial in that fighting, infractions and violence in general have gone down among the 16- and 17-year-olds by having them segregated from 18-year-old inmates.[217]
- In January, 2014, the Humane Alternatives to Long-Term (HALT) Solitary Confinement Act (A08588A / S06466A) was introduced to the New York State Assembly and New York State Senate, respectively.[218] The HALT Solitary Confinement Act would prohibit solitary confinement for youth as well as limit solitary confinement for adults to 15 days, a limit recommended by U.N. Special Rapporteur on Torture, Juan E. Mendez.[219]
- On February 19, 2014, DOCCS entered into stipulation with a group of class action plaintiffs; the stipulation, among other things, provides for increased access to programming and outdoor exercise for 16- and 17- year-old inmates. Among the most important provisions, DOCCS is to offer out-of-cell programming and outdoor exercise to 16- and-

17 year-old inmates, limiting time in their cells to 19 hours a day for five days a week.[220]

- On April 9, 2014, New York Governor Andrew M. Cuomo formed a Commission on Youth, Public Safety & Justice, also known as the "Raise the Age" Commission.[221] In a statement, Governor Cuomo reiterated his support for raising the age of criminal responsibility, announcing that "[i]t's time to improve New York's outdated juvenile justice laws and raise the age at which our children can be tried and charged as adults."[222]
- On August 28, 2014, Mayor de Blasio signed a bill originally introduced by Council Member Dromm that requires the NYC DOC to report on its use of the practice of solitary confinement, including the disclosure of the age, race and gender of anyone subjected to solitary confinement, as well as information about the nature of the infractions.[223]
- According to recent news reports, additional measures in New York City may soon be implemented, including the elimination of punitive segregation of youth at Rikers.[224] According to an internal memorandum that was obtained by The New York Times in late September 2014, Commissioner Ponte has called for the end of solitary confinement for 16- and 17- year-old inmates in New York City prisons by the end of the year.[225] The internal memorandum indicates that solitary confinement will be replaced by "alternative options, intermediate consequences for misbehavior and steps designed to pre-empt incidents from occurring."[226]

On December 1, 2014, the NYC Mayor's office released its Action Plan (Action Plan), detailing the reforms NYC plans to implement regarding the NYC criminal justice system, including with respect to youth.[227]

Among other things, the Action Plan indicates that the City plans to revise the NYC DOC's sentencing guidelines and disciplinary procedures such that alternative sanctions are utilized and disproportionally lengthy sentences are decreased.[228] The Action Plan also indicates that NYC DOC plans to end punitive segregation for adolescents by the end of 2014, but will continue to "deploy punitive segregation in swifter and more targeted ways to cope with serious offenses within a continuum of sanctions."[229]

# SECTION 2: DETRIMENTAL EFFECTS OF SOLITARY CONFINEMENT

## I. Introduction

The use of solitary confinement has extreme and detrimental psychological, physical and developmental effects on adults. These destructive effects are magnified when applied to youth. As Professor Kysel wrote, "[t]he differences between children and adults make young people more vulnerable to harm, and disproportionately affected by the trauma and deprivations of solitary confinement and isolation."[230] Although studies have proven the "negative physiological and psychological reactions to conditions of solitary confinement" for adults, there have been no "systematic studies" of the effect solitary confinement has on youth.[231] Throughout the briefing, numerous presenters relayed first-hand accounts of the deleterious effects that solitary confinement has on virtually every aspect of a young person's well-being. The impact ranges from permanent mental impairment to suicide. The American Academy of Child and Adolescent Psychiatry has stated that:

> The potential psychiatric consequences of prolonged solitary confinement are well recognized and include depression, anxiety and psychosis. Due to their developmental vulnerability, juvenile offenders are at particular risk of such adverse reactions. Furthermore, the majority of suicides in juvenile correctional facilities occur when the individual is isolated or in solitary confinement.[232]

Based on all of these detrimental effects, the American Academy of Child and Adolescent Psychiatry "has concluded that adolescents are in particular danger of adverse reactions to prolonged isolation and solitary confinement and has recommended a ban on the practice."[233]

## II. Mental and Physical Effects of Solitary Confinement on Youth

The use of solitary confinement has been shown to cause or exacerbate mental health problems.[234] Some studies even show the development of adverse psychological symptoms in adults with no history of psychological problems.[235] Dr. Bandy Lee, Assistant Clinical Professor of Psychiatry at Yale

School of Medicine, explained that other cultures "view solitary confinement as a form of torture exceeding that of physical torture,"[236] so stressful that it could trigger major mental illness to a greater extent than genetics or any other factor.[237] As Dr. Lee testified, solitary confinement is considered a risk factor of mental illness because of the neurological and physical effects that can stem from exposure to confinement.[238]

The mental and physical effects of solitary confinement are intensified in the context of youth solitary confinement. The United States Supreme Court has acknowledged that there are differences between adults and children that require special consideration of the mental and physical impact on the latter.[239] Ms. Murtagh opined that the Supreme Court "completely agrees" with scientific research regarding development of the youth's brain, noting that the Court has held that youth lack the culpability of adults because they lack fully developed frontal lobes regulating brain motor control and because their brain structure is fundamentally different from that of adults.[240] As explained in Section 3, the U.S. Supreme Court has held that a youth's age is categorically a mitigating factor in other criminal justice contexts.[241]

Chief Judge of the New York State Court of Appeals Jonathan Lippman has acknowledged the mental differences between youth and adults as well, stating in his annual report:

> Scientific evidence tells us that adolescent brains are not fully matured. In a string of recent cases, the United States Supreme Court has recognized that the parts of their brains that govern reasoning, impulse control and judgment are still developing and, as a result, most adolescents lack the capacity to fully appreciate the consequences of their actions. Moreover, studies indicate that older adolescents, 16- and 17-year-olds whom we now prosecute and sentence in criminal courts, are not only more likely to re-offend and to re-offend sooner, but also go on to commit violent crimes and serious property crimes at a far higher rate than those young people who go through the family court system. Simply put, public safety is not enhanced when we prosecute and punish 16- and 17-year-olds as adults.[242]

The U.S. DOJ's Office of Juvenile Justice and Delinquency Prevention has stated that "isolation of children is dangerous and inconsistent with best practice and that excessive isolation can constitute cruel and unusual punishment."[243] Dr. Lee stressed that the use of solitary confinement for youth produces "life threatening risk[s]" and has negative psychological, neurological, and physical effects on youth.[244]

### *A. Solitary Confinement and Brain Development*

The human body undergoes significant changes during adolescence,[245] including physical development of secondary sex characteristics and development of the brain's frontal lobe.[246] This part of the brain is critical for judgment and impulse control.[247] The frontal lobe is responsible for cognitive processing, such as planning, strategizing, and organizing thoughts and actions.[248] As a result of an adolescent's incomplete brain development, decision-making processes can be impulsive and immature.[249] According to Dr. Venters, the prefrontal cortex of an adolescent's brain does not develop fully until the early 20s.[250] For this reason, multiple presenters recommended that when considering the ban on placing youth in solitary confinement, the term "youth" should be defined as young adults up to the age of 25.[251]

Mr. Paltrowitz agreed, opining that the conversation regarding youth and solitary confinement should consider those up to the age of 25, stating "[a]ge 17 does not draw the line. Somebody who is 17 very quickly becomes 18, becomes 20, becomes 25 and these individuals [sic] should not be subjected to the torture that is solitary confinement."[252] Mr. Paltrowitz concluded that "[w]e need to insure that no young person in their mid-20s ever spends any time in solitary and we need to end solitary for all people and particularly prolonged solitary for all people."[253]

Dr. Lee told the Committee that the brain makes humans highly emotional and vulnerable, especially at developing stages where a negative stimulus or lack of stimulation from the environment can be particularly harmful.[254] Dr. Lee also stated that behavioral evidence shows how such lack of stimulation is far more harmful to an individual than physical, sexual or verbal abuse.[255] Solitary confinement also affects adolescent alexithymia, which is defined as the inability to understand one's own emotions.[256] Specifically, because this ability starts to develop later on in adulthood, adolescents cannot properly determine how they are feeling.[257]

This evidence regarding brain development is particularly alarming given the April 2014 report by the Journal of Adolescent Health which revealed that about half of the 16- to 18-year-olds in NYC DOC facilities had a traumatic brain injury before being incarcerated.[258] The report accompanies another body of research showing that brain injuries are linked to higher rates of breaking jailhouse rules, substance abuse, and greater difficulty re-entering society following prison.[259]

### *B. Solitary Confinement and Mental Health*

According to the American Civil Liberties Union and Human Rights Watch report, *Growing Up Locked Down*, more than 48 percent of adolescents at Rikers have been diagnosed with mental health problems.[260] When taking into consideration those with substance abuse or personality disorders, the number of mentally ill at Rikers could be "at least 90 percent."[261] According to another report by Drs. James Gilligan and Bandy Lee, these numbers increase significantly for adolescents in punitive segregation, with 73 percent of adolescents in solitary confinement being diagnosed as either seriously or moderately mentally ill.[262] The Gilligan-Lee Report also notes that the proportion of mentally ill inmates in New York City jails is the largest it has ever been and continues to grow.[263] In fact, jails and prisons nationwide "have become *de facto* mental health hospitals over the past half-century, in large part as the aftermath and unintended consequences of the de-institutionalization of people with mental illness."[264] The percentage of adolescents diagnosed as seriously or moderately mentally ill in New York City prisons is nearly double the percentage of inmates jail-wide diagnosed with mental illness.[265]

With respect to adolescents, experts on adolescent psychology agree that prolonged exposure to isolation — including solitary confinement — can exacerbate or even cause mental disabilities or other serious health problems.[266] In fact, youth "subjectively perceive time differently so that a sanction of time in solitary for a [youth] is much longer than that . . . same sanction of time for [an] adult."[267] The effect of solitary confinement on the immature brains of youth is strikingly evident, when considering the personal accounts of youth placed in solitary confinement. These isolated youth often describe "losing touch with reality while isolated."[268] Professor Kysel provided details of the mental anguish one 14-year-old experienced while in solitary confinement. This youth stated, "I felt like I was going mad. Nothing but a wall to stare at . . . I started to see pictures in the little bumps. Eventually, I said the hell with it and started acting insane. I made little characters with my hands and acted out video games I used to play on the outside."[269]

Professor Kysel also wrote about his interaction with a young man, who showed him the cuts and scars on his arm from self-harm; this young man also spoke with Professor Kysel about the years of mental anguish he had suffered as a result of his solitary confinement.[270] The young man recounted, "I would hear stuff. When no one was around it was harder to control. When I was by myself, I would hear stuff and see stuff more. . . . [Solitary confinement] is not a place you want to go. . . . It's like mind torture."[271]

Council Member Dromm also described the effects of solitary confinement on a young man who had spent 150 days in solitary confinement:

> The young man emerged from these periods of isolation and deprivation a hollow shell of his former self. Like so many others who have endured extreme and continued isolation he's now withdrawn and anxious and hypersensitive. He has difficulty with concentration and memory and he experiences unpredictable fluctuations in temperament.[272]

As discussed briefly above, Ms. Murtagh told the story of Raymond, who was incarcerated when he was 17, and at the time of the Committee briefing was serving a solitary confinement penalty of 39 months.[273] Raymond reported that the extended time in solitary confinement was "causing [him to have] a mental breakdown."[274]

A youth's ability to control his or her emotions is also negatively impacted by solitary confinement. Council Member Dromm testified about a young man who was subjected to solitary confinement and whose mental "instability makes him susceptible to fits of anger and rage and also nervousness and paranoia. As with countless other formerly isolated inmates, the extent of his cognitive and psychological devastation remains unclear."[275] Another youth subjected to solitary confinement recounted, "I couldn't sleep. I was having anger. My anger was crazy. I was having outbursts."[276]

Many incarcerated youth have previous traumatic experiences. These previous traumas often exacerbate the mental anguish youth experience while in solitary confinement. Professor Kysel referenced the story of a girl who was held in protective custody for three months when she was 15.[277] She said, "When I was eleven, I was raped. And it happened again in 2008 and 2009."[278] She said that when she was isolated, the memories came back: "I was so upset . . . and a lot was surfacing from my past . . . I don't like feeling alone. That's a feeling I try to stay away from. I hate that feeling."[279]

The detrimental mental impact solitary confinement has on youth is often too much for them to bear. Suicide and suicide attempts among youth have a high correlation with their placement in solitary confinement.[280] At New York City's Rikers facility, the accounts of both suicide attempts and self-harm among youth who have been subjected to solitary confinement are harrowing. One young girl subjected to solitary confinement at Rikers recalled:

> I just felt I wanted to die, like there was no way out — I was stressed out. I hung up [tried to hang myself] the first day. I took a sheet and tied it to my light and they came around. . . . The officer, when she was doing

> rounds, found me. She was banging on the window: "Are you alive? Are you alive?" I could hear her, but I felt like I was going to die. I couldn't breathe.[281]

Those who act out because of mental illness are often punished because of it. In perhaps one of the most disheartening portrayals of cruelty, a young girl was actually punished for attempting suicide after hearing of her grandmother's passing.[282] Ms. Hamilton of the Legal Aid Society shared the story of a young girl who was sent to solitary confinement as a result of a minor violation but had her solitary confinement sentence extended as a result of a suicide attempt. The girl suffered from post-traumatic stress disorder and depression — conditions that worsened when she was locked in isolation for 24 hours per day.[283] Her only human contact was the screams she heard from other inmates.[284] When she found out her grandmother died, she took a sheet from her segregation unit and hung it to the sprinkler of the door.[285] The girl reported that "a staff member noticed and when they came into her cell and she refused to stop her suicide attempt she was ripped down and infracted for disobeying a direct order and physically resisting staff."[286]

Mualimm-Ak succinctly summarized his view of the mental health issue regarding youth in solitary confinement stating, "[t]he statistics are that over 44 percent of people incarcerated, juveniles, have some type of mental illness. I can guarantee if you don't go in [to prison] with [a mental illness], you're coming out with it."[287]

Furthermore, oftentimes inmates feel stigma associated with seeking help for mental issues and thus, mental illness often goes untreated. John Perez, a safety advocate from the Mental Health Project of the Urban Justice Center, explained that inmates are "stigmatized, ostracized, made fun of, bullied, extorted, just a host of things that can make your sentence a whole lot more difficult, so even if I do have a mental issue I may not want to address it for fear of all of the interventions or having to deal with the officers."[288]

Pursuant to the SHU Exclusion Law referenced above, those who are diagnosed with serious mental illnesses are not allowed to be placed in solitary confinement for a period greater than 30 days. However, despite the fact that an incarcerated youth may have serious mental health issues, the prison personnel may diagnose the youth with a mere behavioral or personality disorder — a diagnosis that would not trigger the SHU Exclusion Law. Megan Crowe-Rothstein, Director of Social Work at the Urban Justice Center Mental Health Project, reported about a young man who had been previously diagnosed with serious mental health issues (bipolar disorder, substance abuse, mental retardation, and schizophrenia, and chronic suicidal ideation and impulsive mood swings).[289] Despite the young man's previous history of serious mental health issues, his condition was characterized by prison clinicians as mere behavioral and personality issues.[290] This 16-year-old boy was issued a four-month ticket for solitary confinement.[291] Ms. Crowe-Rothstein recalled how the young man wrote letters to her about his plan to commit suicide by overdosing on his psychiatric medication.[292]

The detrimental effects of solitary confinement on youth are not limited to mental effects but also extend to physical effects. The increase in the use of solitary confinement has resulted in an increase in violent and suicidal behaviors.[293] As stated above, suicide attempts are often coupled with self-mutilation. According to data collected by the DOHMH, from 2007 through 2012, the number of self-mutilations and suicide attempts by Rikers inmates increased more than 75 percent.[294] This statistic is particularly telling given that the percentage of punitive segregation beds has increased 70 percent over that same period.[295]

The youth who suffer through solitary confinement are often reduced to mere shells of their former selves. Ms. Murtagh told the story of Richard, who had been "locked in a janitor's closet overnight for . . . three days" and later placed in solitary confinement.[296] Richard wrote, explaining, "I am depressed. Physically I feel weak because I don't get rec[reation] and to be behind this plexiglass all day with no air, it's not circulating. I cannot work out because I get dizzy."[297] After a week, "[Richard] was found unresponsive and drooling in his cell and was taken to the medical unit."[298] Ms. Crowe-Rothstein also recounted the story of another young man incarcerated at Rikers. Ms. Crowe-Rothstein had met the young man while he was in general population, at which time she deemed him to be "easy to talk with . . . smil[ing] a lot."[299] After one week of solitary, Ms. Crowe-Rothstein met with this young man again. At this point "[s]peaking to him became like pulling teeth, he spoke in single-word answers even though he was desperate to receive visitors. He had trouble sleeping, lost weight, and became deeply introverted."[300]

Isolated youth also experience very little in the way of exercise.[301] Professor Kysel noted that youth in solitary confinement were not encouraged to do any type of physical exercise recommended by the U.S. Department of Health and Human Services for teens and if there was any exercise, it took place in small metal cages only a few times per week.[302] A more detailed discussion of barriers to recreation is contained in Section 1, Section II.C.1 (pp. 17–18).

## III. Developmental Effects of Solitary Confinement on Youth

Placing youth in solitary confinement robs them of imperative resources during the critical stages of their social, emotional, and educational development. According to Professor Kysel, the majority of adult jail facilities do not have the specialized programming necessary for a youth's development making "normal growth and development — social, emotional, educational — all but impossible."[303]

### *A. Solitary Confinement and Social and Emotional Development*

Dr. Lee compared human contact to food, as it "is not something that we think much about in its steady presence, however, its absence can be devastating. . . ."[304] Although studies have shown that social interaction for youth is important for their development, "young people in adult jails and prisons reported being denied contact with their families."[305] Various rehabilitative programs show that, for mental health and behavior control, teaching inmates how to socialize is far more effective than confinement.[306] One young person reported on the impact not being able to interact with her family had on her: "It was very depressing not being able to give them a hug, I would cry about that."[307] Another young person noted that "visits behind glass were torture."[308] But in fact, it is these family visits that often give youth the will to live while they are incarcerated.[309]

The absence of contact that characterizes solitary confinement stunts the emotional development of adolescents. As New York City Council Member Dromm said, developing adolescents placed in isolation and forced idleness, with little or no access to meaningful educational, vocational or rehabilitative programing, cannot fully recover from the "trauma of prolonged solitary confinement."[310] NYC BOC Commissioner Judge Hamill stated that "[s]olitary confinement causes harm to a youth's emotional, mental and psychiatric, educational, social, physical health and well-being through the isolation and the forced idleness."[311]

### *B. Solitary Confinement and Educational Development*

The Individuals with Disabilities Education Act[312] (IDEA), gives children with learning disabilities the right to receive specialized education. IDEA requires that institutions develop individualized educational programs (IEPs) for children with special educational needs. Additionally, as described in more detail in Section 3, Section II.A (pp.42), PREA requires isolated youth to have "access to legally-mandated educational programming or special education services."[313] Incarcerated youth, and particularly those in solitary, have little if any opportunity to receive education as they are "prevented from going to school or participating in any activity that promotes growth or change."[314] As Council Member Dromm made clear, it is a violation of the youth's IEP to not provide him or her with education while in solitary confinement.[315]

New York State offers special education and Title I educational programs (basic education skills) for school-age offenders.[316] Any incoming inmate under the age of 21 is evaluated for special education needs and "referred to one of 14 designated Special Education facilities."[317] The Committee on Special Education develops IEPs for youth.[318] Advocates reported to Committee members that youth in solitary confinement in adult prisons in New York State receive, at best, minimal educational instruction. They are not allowed to participate in any group educational activities and instead are supposed to be given "cell study" worksheets. Advocates report that, in many cases, these worksheets are not distributed and that when they are, they are rarely collected for assessment and feedback. Youth have no access to teachers and report that the study sheets serve no real educational purpose.

In New York City, all incarcerated youth at Rikers who are not in solitary confinement attend the East River Academy, which is controlled by the New York City Department of Education.[319] However, adolescents in solitary confinement at Rikers receive minimal education, if any. The Children's Defense Fund (CDF) Written Statement detailed that the educational opportunities while in solitary confinement at Rikers consisted merely of "workbook pages to be completed on their own with minimal access to teachers via a phone brought into their cell, if any."[320] The CDF also noted the fact that "more than 50 percent of the students at Rikers read below a 6th grade level," making it "impossible to imagine [that] these adolescents who are so far behind academically already [can] mak[e] any educational strides while confined in isolation 23 hours a day . . . for periods of time that stretch beyond six full weeks."[321] On the Committee's visit to Rikers, the principal of the East River Academy explained that the youth in solitary confinement received homework weekly in the form of work packets. The young people the members of the Committee spoke with at Rikers reported that the worksheets often took as little as 15 minutes a day to complete, well below the state requirement of 5.5 hours of daily educational instruction. In the best cases, these materials were tailored to the level of the individual student, collected and returned. The Committee also learned from the principal that no IDEA assessments were conducted for incoming juvenile inmates despite Federal requirements to do so.

One incarcerated young person explained the deleterious effects of not having any educational stimuli:

> The only thing left to do is go crazy — just sit and talk to the walls. I catch myself talking to the walls every now and again. It's starting to become a habit because I have nothing else to do. I can't read a book. I work out and try to make the best of it, but there is no best. Sometimes I go crazy and I can't even control my anger anymore. . . . I feel like I am alone, like no one cares about me — sometimes I feel like, why am I even living?[322]

Ms. Freeman told the story of a 16-year-old boy who was prosecuted as an adult and sent to Rikers, ultimately going in and out of solitary confinement for eight months.[323] Ms. Freeman stated that this boy, during his time in solitary confinement, "didn't get any kind of education, didn't get any kind of rehabilitative services," and Ms. Freeman further stated, "really to me that is the ultimate tragedy."[324]

As one presenter, Marybeth Zeman, a transitional counselor at a New York county jail, told the Committee, some prison wardens in other jurisdictions have embraced the "philosophy that the more education that inmates receive and the more access to books the easier the inmates are to manage [and in turn these other prison wardens] chose to use solitary confinement sparingly."[325] Mr. Perez described the importance of obtaining an education in his own development: "I wasn't ready to become a responsible man, come to see my actions in a different light, but education actually made those changes for me."[326]

Ms. Zeman summarized the importance of educational development for youth, contrasting education with the brutal realities of solitary confinement, stating "[e]ducation, books and literacy — they are all about changing life's outcomes. Solitary confinement is about making things far worse, offering no hope for change."[327]

### *C. Solitary Confinement and Transition into Society*

The detrimental effect isolation has on the development of youth extends beyond the confines of the solitary confinement cell. Once released back into society, they are often ill-equipped to cope with life outside of prison. As Angela Browne, a Senior Fellow at the Vera Institute of Justice, reported, adolescent inmates are sent to isolation "for too long with little or no programming," "lack of health and mental health care," and lack of transition back to the community after release, "intensifying the damages, the costs and the negative outcomes" of solitary confinement.[328] During the briefing, Council Member Dromm questioned how we can brutalize individuals through isolation, many of whom have mental health and substance abuse problems, and then "release them back into the streets and back into society."[329] He emphasized that society would be better served by providing young inmates with vocational and educational opportunities,[330] than by causing the lifelong cognitive and psychological impacts of extreme isolation.[331] Similarly, DOCCS Commissioner Annucci shared this concern, citing the difficulties for youth inmates transitioning from solitary confinement to the general prison population, let alone the difficulty they have transitioning back into the community.[332]

## SECTION 3: LEGAL CONTEXT

Although there are international, federal and state laws, regulations and policies that address the use of solitary confinement as it applies generally, there is a dearth of laws and regulations related specifically to youth solitary confinement. The Supreme Court has yet to consider the constitutionality of placing children in solitary confinement; however, the Court has ruled that the Constitution's protections apply differently to children in the criminal justice context because of the legal and developmental differences between children and adults.[333] In cases implicating the juvenile death penalty, life without parole, and custodial interrogations, for example, the Court has held that it is unconstitutional to punish children without acknowledging their age, developmental differences or individual characteristics.[334]

The following sections address the legal protections that apply or could apply to the solitary confinement of youth. Several considerations, including: (i) the special needs of children compared with adults, (ii) the detrimental effects of solitary confinement, and (iii) the current lack of legal protection for children highlight the "great need for strong and unequivocal national and state bans on the solitary confinement of children."[335]

### I. Constitutional Protections

The isolation of youth in solitary confinement implicates three provisions of the U.S. Constitution: the Fifth and Fourteenth Amendments provide youth with procedural and substantive due process protections, and the Eighth

Amendment prohibits "cruel and unusual punishments."[336] The Fourteenth Amendment's due process right is violated when the government's conduct "shocks the conscience."[337] As Professor Kysel emphasized, "[l]aws and practices that subject children to [the] inherently cruel and punitive treatment [of solitary confinement] shock the conscience," [338] and thus should be viewed as violating the Fourteenth Amendment.

To implicate the Eighth Amendment, solitary confinement of youth must be "totally without penological justification," "grossly disproportionate," or "involve the unnecessary and wanton infliction of pain,"[339] and the punishments must not be inconsistent with "the evolving standards of decency that mark the progress of a maturing society."[340] The Eighth Amendment's prohibition on inflicting cruel and unusual punishment on youth also "imposes duties on. . . officials, who must provide humane conditions of confinement [and] must ensure that [confined youth] receive adequate food, clothing, shelter, and medical care, and must 'take reasonable measures to guarantee the safety of the [confined youth].'"[341] As Professor Kysel indicated, there are powerful arguments that youth solitary confinement violates the Eighth Amendment prohibition against cruel and unusual punishment because it is so starkly disproportionate for children as a class, because of the differences between children and adults, as well as because it "manifests indifferences *per se* to such a harmful practice."[342]

The few courts that have considered the rights of incarcerated youth with respect to solitary confinement have noted that the extreme psychological distress solitary confinement places on youth constitutes a violation of the Eighth and/or Fourteenth Amendments. The U.S. District Court for the District of Oregon, for example, held that pretrial isolation of younger children in adult correctional facilities violates their Fourteenth Amendment rights even when done as a "means of protecting them from older children."[343] In the context of a youth training school, the U.S. District Court for the Southern District of New York held that the solitary confinement of a 14-year-old girl for two weeks "violate[d] the Constitution's ban on cruel and unusual punishment."[344] The court in its holding quoted Dr. Joseph D. Noshpitz, who remarked:

> What is true in this case for adults is of even greater concern with children and adolescents. Youngsters are in general more vulnerable to emotional pressures than mature adults; isolation is a condition of extraordinarily severe psychic stress; the resultant impact on the mental health of the individual exposed to such stress will always be serious, and can occasionally be disastrous.[345]

In part based on the expert testimony of Dr. George Lynn Hardman, Staff Psychiatrist, Roxbury Court Clinic, the U.S. District Court for the District of Rhode Island held that isolation of children in a boys' training school violated the Eighth Amendment.[346] Dr. Hardman stated:

> It is my professional opinion that confining a child in isolation for punishment serves no treatment purpose whatsoever. On the contrary, because the child's problem or problems are in no way being dealt with during the period in which he is confined in isolation, the child's behavior deteriorates rather than improves in the course of his isolation. The isolation of a child only inhibits that child's emotional development.[347]

The U.S. District Court for the District of Hawaii, in 2006, held that the use of isolation to protect lesbian, gay, bisexual, or transgender juveniles is "inherently punitive and is well outside the range of accepted professional practices."[348] Additionally, whether the context is juvenile death penalty, juvenile life without parole, or juvenile custodial interrogation, the Supreme Court has held that "punishing or questioning children without acknowledging their age, developmental differences, or individual characteristics is unconstitutional."[349]

As noted earlier in this report, in the latter part of the 19th century, the Supreme Court considered the issue of solitary confinement and "ultimate[ly] reject[ed] . . . it as a means of controlling prisoners."[350] For more than half a century after *In re Medley*, the use of solitary confinement and isolation was out of favor in the United States; however, the "use of solitary [confinement] escalated in the 1980s and 1990s with the construction of freestanding supermax facilities and other units designed with isolation in mind."[351] An example of these supermax facilities is the Ohio State Penitentiary (OSP), which was the subject of a § 1983[352] class action lawsuit brought by prisoners in *Wilkinson* v. *Austin*.[353] In affirming the district court's finding that an inmate had a protected liberty in avoiding assignment at the supermax facility, the Supreme Court described the OSP in the following manner:

> In OSP almost every aspect of an inmate's life is controlled and monitored. Inmates must remain in their cells, which measure 7 by 14 feet, for 23 hours per day. A light remains on in the cell at all times, though it is sometimes dimmed, and an inmate who attempts to shield the light to sleep is subject to further discipline. During the one hour per day that an inmate may leave his cell, access is limited to one of two indoor recreation cells.

> Incarceration at OSP is synonymous with extreme isolation. In contrast to any other Ohio prison, including any segregation unit, OSP cells have solid metal doors with metal strips along their sides and bottoms which prevent conversation or communication with other inmates. All meals are taken alone in the inmate's cell instead of in a common eating area. Opportunities for visitation are rare and in all events are conducted through glass walls. It is fair to say OSP inmates are deprived of almost any environmental or sensory stimuli and of almost all human contact.[354]

Based on this recent description of solitary confinement, Alexander A. Reinert, Professor of Law at the Benjamin N. Cardozo School of Law, told the Committee that "if one considers the . . . evolving standards of decency, one could conclude that both the use of solitary confinement [for youth] and its use for the periods of time common in New York State are in serious tension with Eighth Amendment principles."[355]

## II. Statutory Protections

No state prohibits the solitary confinement of children in adult jails and prisons by statute.[356] Three states — New York, Mississippi and Montana — impose limitations on the use of solitary confinement on youths in adult prisons.[357] Many state juvenile justice agencies have implemented policy changes regulating isolation practices, with a majority limiting isolation to a maximum of five days,[358] and six states — Alaska, Connecticut, Maine, Nevada, Oklahoma and West Virginia — prohibiting solitary confinement in youth facilities by statute.[359]

Additionally, only five states — Delaware, Washington, South Carolina, Michigan, and Pennsylvania — permit solitary confinement as a mode of punishment for criminal law violations.[360] In Delaware, a court may specify that a sentence include solitary confinement, but not for a period of time exceeding 3 months.[361] In Washington, the period may not exceed 20 days.[362] South Carolina generally permits courts to impose a punishment of solitary confinement for felonies in limited circumstances, whereas Michigan empowers a sentencing court to specify that a prisoner be kept in solitary confinement without significant limitations.[363] Pennsylvania is unusual in that it includes solitary confinement as a potential punishment for specific offenses, without apparent limitation on the time frame.[364]

As compared with criminal statutes, laws governing prison discipline vary widely by state.[365] The majority of states make no specific reference to solitary confinement as a disciplinary option for convicted prisoners, but a minority of states explicitly reference solitary confinement by statute.[366] Two states — Louisiana and Wisconsin — explicitly permit the use of solitary confinement without a time limit.[367] Four other states — Massachusetts, Nebraska, South Dakota, and Tennessee — provide time limits for solitary confinement ranging up to a maximum of 30 days.[368] Maine requires that all solitary confinement punishment be approved by the prison's chief administrative officers and that inmates confined for more than one day be visited every 24 hours by medical staff.[369] In county jails, Iowa, Michigan, Minnesota and Wisconsin provide a 10-day time limit; by contrast, New Jersey has no time limit.[370] However, when viewing state statistics as a whole, "there is a near consensus among the States that solitary confinement is inappropriate as a means of criminal punishment."[371]

Professor Reinert has made the argument that prison officials may have less authority to use solitary confinement as a result of state legislative action:

> The argument could be sketched as follows: (1) solitary confinement has been rejected as a permissible punishment for violations of the penal code of nearly every state; (2) violations of prison discipline are by definition less serious than violations of criminal law; and (3) therefore as a matter of proportionality or evolving standards of decency, prison officials may not use as punishment a mode that has been rejected by elected legislatures.[372]

On the federal level, no statute or regulation prohibits solitary confinement of children in youth facilities, jails or prisons.[373] However, the Juvenile Justice and Delinquency Prevention Act (JJDPA) creates financial incentives for states to divert youth out of adult facilities,[374] and other statutes, detailed below, regulate certain aspects of youth isolation.

Aside from the statutes dealing directly with solitary confinement, Ms. Freeman noted that many states including New York require, by statute, mandatory sentencing for certain crimes, which limits judicial discretion over defendants, including youth defendants.[375]

### *A. The Prison Rape Elimination ACT*

The Prison Rape Elimination Act (PREA) includes some restrictions on placing youth in solitary confinement. First, the DOJ regulations implementing PREA require that, while adult jails and prisons "maintain sight, sound and physical separation between youthful inmates and adult inmates," officials should also use their "best efforts to avoid placing youthful inmates in isolation."[376] Second, PREA requires that the adult facilities placing youth in separation or isolation provide the youth "daily large-muscle exercise," "legally required special education services," and "access to other programs and work opportunities to the extent possible."[377] Professor Kysel explained that while these requirements are a step in the right direction, the regulations contain significant gaps that leave children vulnerable to solitary confinement and the harmful conditions associated with prolonged isolation.[378]

In addition to those PREA-implementing rules specifically geared towards the protection of youth inmates from sexual abuse, there are also more general rules and principles designed to insure a safe and orderly detention environment, free from not only the fact — but also the risk — of abuse. These rules require safeguards against retaliation against youth inmates who bring complaints against guards or fellow inmates as well as safeguards against bias in adjudication or investigation of such complaints.[379] Committee members' discussions with advocates, former inmates, and prison officials in New York and elsewhere indicate that these safeguards practically require complaint procedures that substantially protect the anonymity of the complainant, adjudicators and investigators who are insulated from informal pressures by corrections staff, the monitoring of suspicious behavior by corrections staff and fellow inmates, and the capacity of supervisors to deploy personnel to avoid risks associated with such behavior in advance of formal administrative findings of wrong-doing.

### *B. The Civil Rights of Institutionalized Persons Act*

The Civil Rights of Institutionalized Persons Act (CRIPA)[380] gives the U.S. Attorney General the power to institute a civil action against any State, State subdivision, official, employee, or agent thereof that subjects "persons residing in or confined to an institution . . . to egregious or flagrant conditions which deprive such persons of any rights, privileges, or immunities secured or protected by the Constitution or laws of the United States causing such persons to suffer grievous harm."[381] The DOJ recently has used CRIPA to conduct a two-year investigation of Rikers.[382] The recent CRIPA report produced by the DOJ is discussed below.

### *C. Section 14141 of the Violent Crime Control and Law Enforcement Act of 1994*

Section 14141 of the Violent Crime Control and Law Enforcement Act of 1994 (Section 14141) also makes it unlawful for any governmental authority or agent that is responsible for the "administration of juvenile justice or the incarceration of juveniles" to "engage in a pattern or practice of conduct . . that deprives persons of rights, privileges, or immunities secured or protected by the Constitution or laws of the United States."[383] Section 14141 also empowers the U.S. Attorney General to bring civil actions under such circumstances.[384]

## III. International Human Rights

International law and guidelines, while not binding, have often served as a guide for U.S. courts, including the Supreme Court, when determining whether certain practices violate a child's constitutional rights.[385] These international guidelines aid courts and regulatory bodies in determining exactly what are "the evolving standards of decency that mark the progress of a maturing society."[386] According to Professor Kysel, international standards can be useful in determining the contours of constitutional protections for children in solitary confinement in the United States.[387] Both international human rights treaties and human rights organizations have "recognize[d] that children, by reason of their physical and mental immaturity, need special safeguards and care, including appropriate legal protection, before as well as after birth."[388] According to the International Covenant on Civil and Political Rights (ICCPR), a treaty adopted by the United Nations General Assembly and ratified by the United States, youth offenders should be "accorded treatment appropriate to their age and legal status."[389]

Additionally, both the United Nations Committee on the Rights of the Child and the United Nations Rules for the Protection of Juveniles Deprived of Their Liberty state that disciplinary measures for youth such as "closed or solitary confinement" "must be strictly forbidden."[390]

Similarly, the Inter-American Commission on Human Rights has urged the Organization of American States member States, including the United States, to absolutely prohibit the placement of children in solitary confinement "as by definition it constitutes cruel, inhuman, or degrading treatment."[391] Likewise, the Office of the U.N. Special Rapporteur on Torture has repeatedly called for the abolition of solitary confinement of children under age 18.[392]

## IV. Legislative Efforts

### *A. National*

On July 8, 2014, U.S. Sens. Cory Booker (D-NJ) and Rand Paul (R-KY) introduced the REDEEM Act (Record Expungement Designed to Enhance Employment) in Congress.[393] One of the components of the REDEEM Act is to incentivize states to raise the age of criminal responsibility to 18 years old.[394] States that raise the minimum age of original jurisdiction for adult criminal courts to age 18 would be offered preference for Community Oriented Policing Services (COPS) grant applications.[395] The REDEEM Act also seeks to restrict the use of youth solitary confinement to only "the most extreme circumstances in which it is necessary to protect a youth detainee or those around them."[396] Additional components of the REDEEM Act are as follows:

- **Allows for sealing and expunging of youth records:** Provides for automatic expungement of records for youth who commit non-violent crimes before they turn 15 and automatically seals records for those who commit non-violent crimes after they turn 15 years old.
- **Offers adults a way to seal non-violent criminal records:** Presents the first broad-based federal path to the sealing of criminal records for 18-year-olds and older. Non-violent offenders will be able to petition a court and make their case. Furthermore, employers requesting FBI background checks will get only relevant and accurate information — thereby protecting job applicants — because of provisions to improve the background check system.
- **Lifts ban on SNAP and TNAF benefits for low-level drug offenders:** The REDEEM Act restores access to benefits for those who have served their time for use and possession crimes, and for those who have paid their dues for distribution crimes provided their offense was rationally related to a substance abuse disorder and they have enrolled in a treatment program.[397]

### *B. New York*

Currently, neither New York State nor New York City has any statutes that would restrict the use of youth solitary confinement or isolation within prisons.[398] The DOCCS gives "broad powers" to hearing officers to isolate inmates for extended periods of time "with some prisoners spending year after year in isolation."[399] While incarcerated youth in New York City and New

York State are entitled to a disciplinary hearing regarding a punishment of solitary confinement, the youth is afforded no right to counsel at the hearing.[400] According to Ms. Murtagh, should the youth wish to file a grievance, it will likely be denied, noting with respect to the DOCCS process, "[i]f you got a bad decision, most of them do, then it goes to the . . . Central Office Review Committee in Albany, and in 95 percent of these cases we see, if not more, the result is 'we reviewed your grievance, we find it has no merit.'"[401]

As to New York City's system, Ms. Freeman noted, "I believe in the City actually most grievances don't get answered. They just don't answer them."[402] Ms. Murtagh suggested that attorneys should be allowed to file grievances for their youth clients subjected to solitary confinement.[403]

Although there are currently no New York State or New York City statutes protecting youth from solitary confinement, there are legislative efforts underway that address solitary confinement and isolation of youth. These efforts include both New York City and New York State legislation.

**1. New York City**

On August 28, 2014, New York City Mayor Bill de Blasio signed legislation — originally introduced by Council Member Dromm — requiring the NYC DOC to "publish quarterly reports detailing among other things the number of inmates in solitary confinement, their length of stay and whether they were injured or assaulted."[404] At a press conference following the legislation's enactment, NYC DOC Commissioner, Joseph Ponte, lauded the bill's progress towards reform and stated his desire for New York prisons "to rely 'less and less' on solitary confinement in the coming years."[405]

In addition, for over nine months the NYC BOC has been investigating the solitary confinement of youth in NYC jails as part of its rule-making mandate; it will issue a report and promulgate new rules and regulations binding on the city jails.[406] Judge Hamill has indicated that it "is an urgent issue"[407] and acknowledged the "broad consensus" that solitary confinement of youth has a deleterious effect:

> According to the ACLU there is [a] broad consensus that the most effective and developmentally appropriate techniques for managing youth and promoting their healthy growth and development while they are detained requires eliminating solitary confinement, strictly limiting and regulating the use of other forms of isolation and emphasizing positive reinforcement over punishment. For the city jails this means implementing youth-appropriate programming with an incentive system

> expanding recreation, building a community and a culture of respect, the assignment of steady, committed and well trained custodial and clinical staff, and expanding the mental health services so it's available in the general population, which is generally not the case now.[408]

Finally, as noted above, on December 1, 2014, the NYC Mayor's office released the Action Plan, detailing the reforms NYC plans to implement regarding the NYC criminal justice system, including with respect to youth.[409] Under the Action Plan, NYC plans to revise the NYC DOC's sentencing guidelines and disciplinary procedures such that alternative sanctions are utilized and disproportionally lengthy sentences are decreased.[410] The Action Plan also indicates that NYC DOC plans to end punitive segregation for adolescents by the end of 2014, but will continue to "deploy punitive segregation in swifter and more targeted ways to cope with serious offenses within a continuum of sanctions."[411] Based on the Clinical Alternative to Punitive Segregation (CAPS) model, under the Action Plan the NYC DOC and DOHMH will establish Program for Accelerated Clinical Effectiveness (PACE) units that will provide "more intensive and frequent mental health care for people with acute mental health issues."[412] Under the Action Plan, the NYC DOC will also provide eight hours of additional training to officers regarding managing individuals with mental health issues.[413]

As it relates to adolescents, under the Action Plan the NYC DOC will increase officer training regarding trauma-informed best care practices in crisis management, reduce the officer-to-inmate ratio to 1:15 for adolescent units, and physically improve the Rikers School, including installing cameras.[414] Within six months, NYC DOC and DOHMH plan to implement substance use disorder treatment programs, including establishing curricula and recommendations that meet nationwide best practices.[415] Finally, under the Action Plan, NYC DOC plans to immediately expand programming in all jails, including vocational, educational, and discharge planning services in an effort to reduce "idle time and violence."[416]

### 2. New York State

In January, 2014, New York State Assembly Member Jeffrion Aubry and New York State Senator Bill Perkins introduced the Humane Alternatives to Long-Term (HALT) Solitary Confinement Act (A08588A / S06466A) in the New York State Assembly and New York State Senate, respectively.[417] The HALT Solitary Confinement Act would prohibit solitary confinement for youth and for "the elderly, pregnant women, LGBTI individuals, and those with physical or mental disabilities."[418] The law would also limit solitary confinement for adults to 15 days—a limit recommended for adults by U.N. Special Rapporteur on Torture, Juan E. Mendez.[419] For those who present a serious threat to prison safety and need to be separated from the general population for longer periods of time, the law would create new Residential Rehabilitation Units (or RRUs), which are described as "separate, secure units with substantial out-of-cell time, and programs and treatment aimed at addressing the underlying causes of behavioral problems."[420] Senator Perkins stated at a May 5, 2014 HALT Solitary Confinement Act press conference, "Solitary confinement makes people suffer without making our prisons safer. It is counter-productive as well as cruel."[421]

In addition, on April 9, 2014, New York Governor Andrew M. Cuomo formed a Commission on Youth, Public Safety & Justice, also known as the "Raise the Age" Commission.[422] Governor Cuomo reiterated his support for raising the age of criminal responsibility, announcing that "[i]t's time to improve New York's outdated juvenile justice laws and raise the age at which our children can be tried and charged as adults."[423] Governor Cuomo also recognized that New York is one of only two states that charge 16- and 17-year-olds as adults, stating that "[i]t's not right and it's not fair."[424]

## V. Litigation Efforts

On February 19, 2014, DOCCS entered into stipulation with a group of class action plaintiffs, which, among other things, will require DOCCS to place 16- and 17-year-old inmates with long SITU sentences in an alternative form of housing and will limit time in any in-cell confinement to 19 hours a day for youth inmates.[425]

The lawsuit, brought by *pro se* plaintiff Leroy Peoples in April 2011, seeks remedies for his time in solitary confinement.[426] The case was converted into a class action alleging that the long periods of time spent in deplorable conditions in isolation as punishment for misbehavior that involved no violence and no threat to the safety or security of others was grossly disproportionate to the infraction, and therefore unconstitutional.[427] Plaintiffs further alleged that these policies resulted in nearly 70,000 individuals being subjected to extreme isolation sentences in New York State from 2007 to 2011 alone.[428]

The Court-approved stipulation provides for alternatives to solitary confinement sanctions for youth.[429] Importantly, 16- and 17-year-old inmates with long SITU sentences (over 30 days) will be placed in separate alternative housing units.[430] Even under the most restrictive form of disciplinary housing, DOCCS is to provide "out-of-cell programming and outdoor exercise, limiting time in their cells to nineteen (19) hours a day" for five days a week.[431] DOCCS is also to make efforts to house 16- and 17-year-olds in separate facilities from the rest of the population.[432]

During the July 10 briefing, one of the plaintiffs' lawyers in the *Peoples* v. *Fischer* litigation, Alexander Reinert, explained the impact of the litigation. Professor Reinert noted that aside from the provisions specific to youth, the interim agreement provides that the parties will engage in an expert collaborative process to seek reforms to provide for the safety and security of inmates, while improving the conditions for — and limiting the use of — solitary confinement.[433]

In addition, the settlement contains guidance for length of isolation for particular categories of infractions.[434] Specifically, the settlement provides that policies shall be implemented to require: (i) "Tier Review Officers [to] document reasons for any decision to assign a disciplinary violation other than to the lowest possible tier," (ii) "a presumption against consecutive confinement sanctions for violations that arise from the same event absent exceptional circumstances," (iii) "guidelines for the application of second and third infractions of a particular rule only where the subsequent infraction occurs within a specified time after the original incident," and (iv) "discretion for hearing officers to depart upward . . . in appropriate circumstances that are articulated by the hearing officer and referred to Central Office."[435] Professor Reinert also noted that (i) the interim stipulation still permits juveniles to be housed in SHU-type isolation for up to two days a week and (ii) "even if that isolation would not be described as 'solitary' or 'extreme isolation' — 19 hours a day in one's cell is still a form of isolation, and one can expect that it poses risks of harm to some juveniles."[436]

*Peoples* only addresses some issues regarding isolation in New York State prisons. Ms. Murtagh noted that even after implementation, the youth that are sentenced to disciplinary confinement in DOCCS facilities will still be locked in their cells for 19 hours a day during the week and 23 hours a day over the weekend, and there will still be lengthy sentences of in-cell confinement.[437]

Ms. Murtagh further opined that "when I look at the *Peoples* settlement I think it's like attempting to right a capsized ship and sometimes it works and sometimes we should let that ship sink and we should start all over again and in this case, I think we should start all over again."[438] In Ms. Murtagh's opinion, "24 hours a day in general population should be the norm as opposed to talking about isolation as the norm and patting ourselves on the back that now we are at 19 hours a day of isolation instead of 23."[439]

## VI. Executive Efforts

### *A. Department of Justice*

The DOJ has not issued any guidelines or made any statements prohibiting youth from being placed in isolation or solitary confinement.[440] The DOJ, however, has issued reports and made statements indicating that isolation is not an appropriate "remedy" to be imposed on youth. United States Attorney General Eric Holder has stated that in the context of youth with disabilities "[s]olitary confinement can be dangerous, and a serious impediment to the ability of youth to succeed once released."[441] And, as noted in Section 1, the DOJ Standards for the Administration of Juvenile Justice recommends that youth be held in isolation for no longer than 24 hours.[442]

In 2009, the DOJ investigated the Westchester County Jail as well as the Erie County Holding Center and the Erie County Correctional Facility (collectively, "Erie County Facilities").

After its investigation of the Westchester County Jail, having found unconstitutional conditions, the DOJ issued a letter, among other things, directing that Westchester County Jail Isolation Confinement:

- Develop alternative disciplinary actions for juveniles violating institutional rules that result in appropriate time in isolation confinement.
- Ensure that health-care staff are involved in developing and implementing treatment plans for juveniles facing isolation confinement.
- Ensure that juveniles held in the SHU have access to programs appropriate for juveniles.
- Provide greater interaction with jail staff and more rehabilitative programming for juveniles, including those who have committed disciplinary infractions.
- Ensure that juvenile inmates undergo mental health evaluations that address the special developmental needs of adolescents.
- Ensure that juvenile inmates undergo mental health evaluations at regular intervals even if they are not receiving psychotropic medications.

- Ensure that all juvenile inmates are provided housing that maintains sight and sound separation from adult inmates.
- Establish a process for routinely obtaining signed consent forms from the parent or guardian of any juvenile receiving prescribed medications or health care treatment unless otherwise permitted by state or local laws.[443]

In addition, the DOJ entered into two settlement agreements with Erie County to remedy "systemic constitutional violations in the areas of suicide prevention, mental health and medical care, excessive force and protection from harm, and environmental safety."[444]

As discussed above, the United States Attorney's Office for the Southern District of New York issued a CRIPA report to Mayor Bill de Blasio, NYC DOC Commissioner Joseph Ponte, and New York Corporation Counsel Zachary Carter on the treatment of adolescent male inmates at Rikers, finding, among other things, that the NYC "DOC relies far too heavily on punitive segregation as a disciplinary measure, placing adolescent inmates — many of whom are mentally ill — in what amounts to solitary confinement at an alarming rate and for excessive periods of time."[445]

Finally, the Office of Juvenile Justice and Delinquency Prevention (OJJDP), an agency of the DOJ, recently commissioned the National Research Council (NRC) to publish two reports regarding reforming the juvenile justice system. These reports represent an effort by the OJJDP to reform the juvenile justice system and to base this reform on, among other things, scientific evidence related to the physical development of adolescent brains. The first report — *Reforming Juvenile Justice: A Developmental Approach* — was published in 2013 and presented recommendations regarding reforming the juvenile justice system utilizing a scientific approach to comprehending adolescent development.[446] NRC published a second report — *Implementing Juvenile Justice Reform: The Federal Role* — in 2014 to "provide specific guidance to OJJDP regarding the steps that it should take, both internally and externally, to facilitate juvenile justice reform grounded in knowledge about adolescent development."[447]

### *B. Federal Bureau of Prisons*

On February 4, 2014, Sen. Dick Durbin (D-IL), chair of the Senate Judiciary Subcommittee on the Constitution, Civil Rights, and Human Rights, announced that the Federal Bureau of Prisons had "agreed to a comprehensive and independent assessment of its use of solitary confinement in the nation's federal prisons."[448] The Federal Bureau of Prisons' review of solitary confinement is the "first-ever" conducted by the entity.[449] On February 25, 2014, the Senate Judiciary Subcommittee on the Constitution, Civil Rights, and Human Rights conducted a hearing entitled "Reassessing Solitary Confinement II: The Human Rights, Fiscal, and Public Safety Consequences."[450] During the hearing, Sen. Durbin made a statement "calling for all federal and state facilities to end the use of solitary confinement for juveniles, pregnant women, and individuals with serious and persistent mental illness, except in those exceptional circumstances where public safety requires it."[451]

## VII. Other Efforts & Recommendations

In addition to the efforts of regulatory bodies to prohibit solitary confinement of youth, there are various other organizations addressing this issue as well. The Prisoners' Rights Project of the Legal Aid Society (LAS) formed the umbrella group NYC Jails Action Coalition (JAC).[452] The LAS reported to the Committee that JAC had petitioned the NYC BOC to implement new rules regarding isolated confinement to be made part of the jail Minimum Standards.[453] The petition led NYC DOC to make some minimal reforms and led the NYC DOHMH to conduct a study of isolated confinement and the risk of self-harm.[454]

LAS has also called for NYC DOC to develop "alternative disciplinary sanctions" that "do not involve lengthy isolation."[455] LAS believes that the DOJ recommendations for solitary confinement reforms related to 16- to 18-year-old inmates, should also be applied to 18- to 25- year-old inmates, because of the voluminous evidence that brain development continues through age 25.[456] Instead of solitary confinement, LAS suggests that incarcerated youth should be managed by use of room confinement together with mental health intervention.[457] LAS further recommends that prosecution and incarceration of youth should be a last resort and any charges that are brought against youth should be brought in the youth justice system, which has rehabilitative features.[458]

Ms. Murtagh also highlighted the need for a "multidisciplinary review" of DOCCS activities as it relates to solitary confinement and specifically suggested that DOCCS develop transition plans for transfer from solitary confinement to general population for anyone under the age of 25 and those that may have been placed in solitary confinement before they turned 25.[459]

Suggesting that DOCCS move away from solitary confinement, Ms. Murtagh also recommended that "juveniles [are provided] with attorneys at their hearings . . . [and that] the amount of time juveniles can be placed in cell confinement" be "severely limit[ed]."[460]

Professor Ellen Yaroshefsky of Cardozo Law School has made additional proposals in *Rethinking Rikers: Moving from a Correctional to a Therapeutic Model for Youth.*[461] Similar to LAS's proposal, the report suggests that solitary confinement of youth should be eliminated in favor of a therapeutic approach dedicated to youth rehabilitation.[462] Another group, the Council of Juvenile Correctional Administrators' Performance-based Standards (PbS), has called for using isolation only to protect children from themselves or others and if used, isolation should be brief and supervised.[463]

Mr. Paltrowitz noted that the Correctional Association of New York recommends the creation of alternative units where inmates who pose a risk could be separated from the general population but would be allowed access to one hour of recreation and six hours of programming or therapy per day.[464] Mr. Paltrowitz also recommended that solitary confinement extend no more than 15 days, if it has to exist.[465]

Finally, in January 2013, the House of Delegates of the New York State Bar Association called for an end to the use of solitary confinement for children. The report and resolution called for all jails and prisons in New York State to "profoundly restrict the use of long-term solitary confinement, by adopting clear and objective standards to ensure that inmates are separated from the general prison population only in very limited and very legitimate circumstances and only for the briefest period and under the least restrictive conditions practicable."[466] The report cites the recommendation of the Special Rapporteur of the United Nations on Torture that solitary confinement in excess of 15 days should be completely eliminated.[467]

## SECTION 4: FINDINGS AND RECOMMENDATIONS OF THE COMMITTEE

In this report, the New York Advisory Committee has outlined the solitary confinement of youth inmates in New York. Based on the presentations, written statements the Committee has received on the topic from a diverse cross-section of experts — including from New York prison officials — and the Committee's visit to the Rikers Island Correctional Facility, the Committee finds:

**Minority Youth are Disproportionately Subjected to Solitary Confinement**

- In New York, a significant number of youth in state, city, and local prisons are subjected to solitary confinement.
- New York is one of only two states that subjects 16- and 17- year-olds automatically to adult criminal responsibility, with criminal responsibility beginning, for certain serious felonies, as early as age 13. Because 16- and 17- year-olds are subjected to adult criminal responsibility in the judicial system in New York, a greater proportion of youth are subject to solitary confinement. New York should raise the age of criminal responsibility to 18.
- Black inmates are also disproportionately subjected to solitary confinement, making up 49.5 percent of the New York State general prison population, 59 percent of the extreme isolation population but only 17.6 percent of the New York State population.
- Blacks and Hispanics are disproportionately represented in New York prisons, and an astounding 90 to 95 percent of the youth sent to prison in New York City are children of color.

**Solitary Confinement Has a Devastating Effect on Youth**

- Youth inmates committed to solitary confinement are subjected to abhorrent conditions, including: (i) an isolated, sometimes filthy, six-by-eight-square foot cell for 22 to 24 hours a day for weeks or months at a time; (ii) deprivation of physical activity, human and family interaction, and education; (iii) food deprivation; and (iv) deprivation of adequate mental health treatment.
- Solitary confinement has devastating effects on youth, including: (i) exacerbating any existing mental health problems; (ii) increasing the risk of self-harm and suicide; (iii) causing serious deterioration of physical health; and (iv) stunting social, emotional and physical development. While the reforms announced in February 2014 as a part of the *Peoples* v. *Fischer* litigation are a step in the right
- direction, they do not prohibit New York State from housing youth in SITU-type isolation for up to two days a week, they permit in-cell

confinement of up to 19 hours a day, and they do not apply to city and county facilities in the State of New York.

- Given the testimony on brain development and the impact solitary confinement has on mental health, solitary confinement is not an acceptable punishment or discipline strategy for anyone under 25 years old.

**Federal Law Requires Safeguards That Reduce the Risk of Abuse in Confinement**

- Compliance with PREA requires safeguards that reduce the risk of any abuse, whether sexual or non-sexual, by staff or fellow inmates. Jurisdictions outside of New York (i) treat the reduction in liability from adopting such practices and safeguards as cost savings that offset such safeguards' costs and (ii) avoid the costs of complying with PREA by keeping youth inmates out of adult facilities, through insuring that their sentencing courts have discretion to transfer minors out of the adult criminal system and into family court.
- Compliance with PREA requires special safeguards for youth inmates, including assignment of such inmates to housing units by specially trained counselors using tools validated for minors; mechanisms for inmates' filing of complaints and tips in which inmates have confidence because they preserve inmate anonymity; direct access to third-party providers of counseling services such as rape crisis centers; adjudication and investigation procedures by staff separate and distinct from corrections officers at the correctional facility; and capacity of the facility to transfer expeditiously corrections staff suspected of abuse to positions within the facility where they cannot intimidate or retaliate against complainants pending resolution of complaints.

The DOJ is charged with ensuring the fair and impartial administration of justice for all. Under federal statutes, including CRIPA and Section 14141, the DOJ has the statutory authority to commence civil actions to effect changes to the confinement of youth in New York. As a result, the Committee recommends to the Commission the following:

1. The DOJ should use its enforcement powers to as expeditiously as possible require New York state, county and city jails and prisons to adopt the following:

- Eliminate the solitary confinement of inmates under the age of 18 immediately.
- Eliminate the solitary confinement of inmates between the ages of 19 and 25 immediately.
- Undertake a review of all cases of those under age 25 currently being held in solitary confinement and develop a transition plan for each to facilitate expeditious transfer to the general population.
- Transfer any inmates under the age of 25 who are deemed to be particularly vulnerable or otherwise at risk to an alternative housing unit that is equipped to address their special needs and ensure their well-being.

2. The DOJ should use its enforcement powers to require New York state, county, and city jails and prisons to implement alternatives to solitary confinement. Such alternatives should include the following:

- Youth who are a danger to others or themselves should be separated from others in a regular cell and immediately be evaluated by a well-trained mental health professional. These youth should be allowed access to at least one hour of recreation and six hours of programming and/or therapy per day.
- No in-cell segregation of youth should exceed 24 hours, no inmate should be segregated for consecutive 24-hour periods, and no inmate should be segregated more than twice in any two-week period.
- Each housing unit should maintain a committee, comprised of at least a correction officer, a counselor, a mental health professional, an education professional, and the warden or his or her designee, who will design programming for youth inmates so that they have at least one hour of true recreation and at least six hours of out-of-school programming per day with special programming developed for those who are undergoing limited 24-hour in-cell confinement. The committee should also ensure that the programming is implemented consistently and well, and that all youth inmates have the opportunity to fully access the programming, with special programming developed for those who are undergoing limited 24- hour in-cell confinement.

- During in-cell confinement of any kind, New York should mandate that those under 25 years of age continue to receive adequate nutrition, education, vocational training, congregate religious services, exercise, visitation privileges, commissary buys, medical and mental health care and counseling. These enhanced programming and activities should especially be offered on the evening and weekends in order to engage the youth and reduce idleness and should include all youth under age 25, not just those in school programs. Jails and prisons should also encourage and facilitate the involvement of family whenever possible. Although the implementation of enhanced programming may seem costly, such programs are more likely to rehabilitate youth inmates than the current offerings, thereby reducing recidivism in the long run.
- Any segregated young inmate should receive immediate counseling from a trained professional and should be evaluated by a well-trained mental health professional. The professionals should make immediate recommendations to the warden on appropriate housing for the inmate. The general population should also have access to well-trained mental health professionals.

3. The DOJ should use its enforcement powers to require all New York state, county and city jails and prisons to publish data on the use of in-cell confinement for inmates under age 25 on a rolling weekly basis (posted to an easy access website within five days of the end of the week). The reporting should include: (i) the number of inmates in in-cell confinement, (ii) the nature of each infraction resulting in in-cell confinement, (iii) the duration of confinement, (iv) the number of times in any month that an inmate has been in in-cell confinement, (v) the gender, race and age of each inmate in in-cell confinement and (vi) the number of inmates receiving mental health treatment.

4. The DOJ should use its enforcement powers to require all correction officers in both NYC DOC and DOCCS facilities to be provided with regular, comprehensive and effective competency-based training on working with youth detained in jails or prisons, as the DOJ advocated to New York City in its August 4, 2014 letter to NYC Mayor Bill de Blasio, NYC DOC Commissioner Joseph Ponte, and New York Corporation Counsel Zachary Carter. The training should include, but not be limited to, the following: (i) adolescent development, (ii) best practices for working with detained youth, (iii) conflict resolution and crisis intervention and (iv) ways to interact with and manage youth with mental illnesses or suicidal tendencies.

5. The DOJ should use its enforcement powers to require New York state, city and county jails and prisons to implement the directives of PREA. Such changes should include the following:

- Ceasing the practice of incarcerating youth offenders under the age of 18 with adult inmates;
- Ensuring that the assignment of youth inmates to housing facilities are performed by counselors with training in mental health using tools validated for youth. Such assignments should ensure, for example, that LGBT inmates are not assigned solely based on genitalia but rather are based on assessment of both the inmates' preferred gender identification, objective risk and subjective sense of security.
- Ensuring that youth inmates can submit genuinely anonymous complaints to "a public or private entity or office that is not part of the agency, and that is able to receive and immediately forward inmate reports of sexual abuse and sexual harassment to agency officials, allowing the inmate to remain anonymous upon request."[468] Access to a telephone to report misconduct, alone, is not sufficient. To the extent that such calls are monitored, they provide no assurance of confidentiality and are unavailable to inmates in punitive segregation. Instead, inmates should be given access to offices outside the detention facility such as the NYC Bureau of Inspections through media such as e-mail, telephone lines, locked complaint boxes, J-Pay kiosks, or other contacts that provide, through their physical location and other aspects, genuine assurances of confidentiality. Such mechanisms should be available to inmates in in-cell confinement, administrative segregation, or other special housing arrangements.
- Requiring all jails and prisons to use administrative adjudicators, who are genuinely independent of the corrections officers who write infraction tickets to insure that "[t]he credibility of an alleged victim, suspect, or witness shall be assessed on an individual basis and shall not be determined by the person's status as inmate or staff."[469] Safeguards to insure such independence include use of hearing officers who are not uniformed corrections officers but instead civilian staff outside the chain of the detention facility's command. Such staff should receive training designed to prevent bias against complainants based on inmate status.
- Requiring all allegations of sexual abuse to be investigated by staff in a specialized independent investigative unit trained to interrogate

youth appropriately, such as a separate sex crimes unit of the Inspector General's office;

- Giving facility supervisors the power to transfer staff to positions where they will not have contact with persons against whom they are suspected of retaliating or abusing, in situations in which they have credible evidence that a staff member has engaged in abusive or retaliatory behavior. Such power should not require a formal administrative finding of misconduct but should be available while complaints, including anonymous complaints, are pending. Collective action agreements between city and state governments and jail and prison staff should not be grounds for subjecting youth inmates to facilities where they could be subject to intimidation by the staff members against whom they have made allegations.
- Requiring procedures whereby hearing officers who adjudicate allegations of abuse against a staff member or, alternatively, review infractions alleged against a youth inmate, have access to the record of prior complaints and reports by staff involved in the hearing.[470], and;
- Requiring data on prior complaints of abuse by staff be made available to the hearings officers adjudicating such complaints. Those hearings officers should be full-time administrative law judges rather than labor arbitrators jointly appointed by employee organizations and prison authorities. All such data should be reported to a civilian agency independent from corrections facilities or staff, such as the NYC BOC.

6. To the extent the solitary confinement of any inmates under age 25 remains in effect, the DOJ should use its enforcement powers to require New York state, city and county jails and prisons to implement the following:

- Limit the amount of time an inmate can spend in solitary confinement to 15 days in any two month period.
- Require a school age inmate's access to education to continue during solitary confinement, including by teachers being required to spend time with the youth.
- Provide youth under 25 years of age with attorneys at any hearing that can result in in-cell confinement.
- Eliminate the policy that requires an inmate to carry a debt of time owed in solitary confinement if they return to jail or prison.

- Mandate that those under 25 years of age continue to receive adequate nutrition, education, vocational training, congregate religious services, exercise, visitation privileges, commissary buys, medical and mental health care, and counseling during solitary confinement. These activities and enhanced programming should especially be offered in the evening and on weekends in order to engage the youth and reduce idleness and should include all youth under the age of 25, not just those in school programs.
- Ensure that youth inmates with mental illnesses receive proper treatment and are not subjected to solitary confinement. These treatment plans should be developed by well-trained mental health staff. Jails and prisons should also take care to establish therapeutic and secure settings to house youthful inmates with serious mental illnesses who commit rule infractions. These therapeutic and secure settings should be staffed by personnel qualified in youth psychology.
- Require that any inmate under the age of 25 serving a sentence in solitary confinement be given the option to have at least two hours of time outside of his or her cell every day. Given the small number of inmates who take recreation time, recreation should be made available during daylight hours and communicated with an initial clear and loud announcement and subsequent cellby-cell canvassing by a correction officer.
- Publish data on the use of solitary confinement for inmates under age 25 on a rolling weekly basis (posted to an easy access website within five days of the end of the week). The reporting should include: (i) the number of inmates in solitary confinement, (ii) the nature of each infraction resulting in solitary confinement, (iii) the duration of confinement, (iv) the number of times in any month that an inmate has been in solitary confinement, (v) the gender, race and age of each inmate in solitary confinement and (vi) the number of inmates receiving mental health treatment. The results should be used to eliminate the racial disparity between youth of color in solitary confinement and other inmates.
- Create detailed descriptions of the types of infractions for which solitary confinement of inmates under the age of 25 can be imposed. Inmates and prison staff should be educated and trained on these infractions.
- As advocated in the U.S. Department of Justice's August 4, 2014 letter to NYC Mayor Bill de Blasio, NYC DOC Commissioner Joseph

Ponte, and New York Corporation Counsel Zachary Carter, all correction officers in both NYC DOC and DOCCS facilities should be provided with regular, comprehensive and effective competency-based training on working with adolescents detained in jails in prisons. The training should include, but not be limited to the following: (i) adolescent development, (ii) best practices for working with detained youth, (iii) conflict resolution and crisis intervention and (iv) ways to interact with and manage youth with mental illnesses or suicidal tendencies.

- Publish data on a quarterly basis regarding the impact solitary confinement has for inmates under age 25 on: (i) jail and prison costs, (ii) facility safety, (iii) incidents of self-harm, (iv) recidivism, (v) inmate educational level, and (vi) inmate mental health status.
- Develop specific protocols to implement the Committee's recommendations.

7. The DOJ should audit the population classifications for individuals sentenced to solitary confinement.

**Dissent by Robert Paquette**

More than seven years ago, I was given the task of formulating a mission statement for an organization dedicated to educational reform. I took the job most seriously because I believed then — and continue to believe now — that mission statements not only provide indispensable grounding and conceptual boundaries for any institution, but become crucial points of reference, especially at difficult moments, in making tough choices about what is permissible within the organization. When I first arrived on the NYAC committee in 2013, I took a long, hard look at the mission statement on the USCCR's website: "Established as an *independent, bipartisan, fact-finding federal agency*," it reads, "our mission *is to inform the development of national civil rights policy* and *enhance enforcement of federal civil rights laws. We pursue this mission by studying alleged deprivations* of voting rights and *alleged discrimination based* on race, color, religion, sex, age, disability, or national origin, or in the administration of justice. *We play a vital role in advancing civil rights through objective and comprehensive investigation, research, and analysis* on issues of fundamental concern to the federal government and the public." [My emphasis]

In examining the report "Civil Rights Implications of Solitary Confinement of Youth in New York," my standard of evaluation was the charge given to committee members by the mission statement and by the language of the 1957 Civil Rights Act, which created the Commission, as well as by the Civil Rights Act of 1994, which amended the original act. I could not vote for the report for several reasons. I can only state a few here. The report does not represent, in my view "objective and comprehensive investigation" in a "bi-partisan" fashion. The report, in attempting to make the case for juvenile solitary confinement as a form of civil rights discrimination, focuses on age as well as race/ethnicity. Yet, at a previous meeting of the NYAC committee early in the process of investigating this issue, I raised the question of age and was told without a murmur of dissent that under the Civil Rights acts, the kind of age discrimination the committee was charged to consider was age discrimination in employment of those forty or over, consistent, I believe, with the 1967 Age Discrimination in Employment Act. Indeed, a USCCR webpage, which is headed "Getting Uncle Sam to Enforce Your Civil Rights," states explicitly, "Discrimination is illegal when an individual is denied an opportunity or a service based on . . . age, which refers to persons aged 40 or over."

My dissent from the committee report also centers on language and standards of comparison that seem tendentious to me. An "objective, fact-finding" report would address evidence that runs counter to the string of advocates whose words are extensively quoted in the report. Rikers has special problems, but its culture is not that of, say, Marcy Correctional in upstate New York. Nowhere does the report examine the role of juvenile solitary confinement as seen through the eyes of the guards or their union representatives who must face life threatening situations and facilities that typically do not lend themselves to idyllic solutions. One member of the committee raised the question of whether the report could be seen as balanced and fair-minded without statistical information on the race-ethnicity of those committing crimes. A balanced and objective report would provide such information and subject it to fair-minded analysis. In my view, the overwhelming evidence about the impact of solitary confinement on mental health coupled with the extraordinarily high proportion of juvenile offenders with mental illness argues for a report that focuses on, in the words of the USCCR, "disability, which refers to physical or mental impairments that substantially limit one or more major life activities of an individual."

**Dissent by Peter Wood**

I voted against the adoption of New York Advisory Committee's report, "The Civil Rights Implications of Solitary Confinement of Youth in New York." I believe the report rests on invalid premises and that its recommendations are deeply flawed.

Solitary confinement may or may not be wise penal policy, but the report fails to establish that its use in New York State violates "civil rights" as defined by the mandate for the U.S. Civil Rights Commission. The committee reached for three justifications for treating solitary confinement as a civil rights issue. The first is that solitary confinement has a "disparate impact" on minority groups. The report's "disparate impact" theory works from the raw percentage of minority members who spend time in solitary confinement, and pays no attention at all to how this number compares to the percentage of minority individuals who are incarcerated. If the percentage of the minority inmates in jail or prison who spend time in solitary were higher than the percentage of minority inmates overall, there could be a case for "disparate impact," but the report does not even attempt to establish this.

Second, the report asserts that solitary confinement discriminates against youthful offenders and is therefore a form of age discrimination. This theory is based on the observation that the human brain's frontal lobe continues to develop up [to] the age of 25. The frontal lobe is the seat of executive functions such as planning, working memory, and impulse control. The Advisory Committee, however, overreaches. The volume of gray matter in the frontal lobe peaks at age 11 in girls and at age 12 in boys. The brain then gradually "prunes" connections and grows more efficient. This brain maturation surely has important behavioral correlates, but we are a long way from a scientific finding that adolescents or adults in their early 20s are incapable of prudential judgment or self-control, and very far indeed from the speculative hypothesis that solitary confinement poses a special risk to those under age 25. According to the Journal of Adolescent Health, "Many neuroscientists argue that empirical support for a causal relationship between neuromaturational processes and real-world behavior is currently lacking."

Third, the committee asserts that solitary confinement violates the Eighth Amendment's ban on "cruel and unusual punishments." The "Eighth Amendment" theory is suppositious. Solitary confinement is by no stretch "unusual," having been widely practiced in the United States for over two centuries. Numerous high court rulings have found it an acceptable part of penal policy. Properly administered, it is no crueler than other forms of confinement. It can be, of course, improperly administered in a manner that is undoubtedly cruel, but that isn't the position that this committee has adopted. Rather, it presents solitary confinement as essentially cruel.

The committee's thirty recommendations, to the extent they are based on these premises, are invalid. As the "findings" present the disparate impact, age discrimination, and Eighth Amendment arguments as central, I find the report fundamentally unreliable.

## End Notes

[1] *See generally* THE PEW CENTER ON THE STATES, ONE IN 100: BEHIND BARS IN AMERICA (2008), [hereinafter ONE IN 100], *available at* http://www.pewtrusts.org/~/media/legacy/uploadedfiles/pcs_assets/2008/one20in20100pdf.pdf (last accessed Oct. 21, 2014).

[2] J.F., *Why Does America Have Such a Big Prison Population?*, THE ECONOMIST (Apr. 14, 2013), *available at* http://www.economist.com/blogs/economist-explains/2013/08/economist-explains-8 (last accessed Oct. 21, 2014).

[3] INTERNATIONAL CENTRE FOR PRISON STUDIES, WORLD PRISON POPULATION LIST (10th ed. 2011), *available at* http://www.prisonstudies.org/sites/prisonstudies.org/files/resources/downloads/wppl_10.pdf (last accessed Oct. 21, 2014).

[4] Bandy Lee, testimony, Briefing Before the U.S. Commission on Civil Rights, briefing, New York, NY, July 10, 2014, transcript, p. 156 [hereinafter Briefing Transcript].

[5] ONE IN 100, p. 5.

[6] *See* TRENDS IN U.S. CORRECTIONS, THE SENTENCING PROJECT 3 (2013), *available at* http://www.sentencingproject.org/doc/publications/inc_Trends_in_Corrections_Fact_sheet.pdf (last accessed Oct. 21, 2014).

[7] *Id.*

[8] *Id.*

[9] *Id.* p. 5.

[10] *Id.*

[11] *See* Lisa Freeman, Briefing Transcript, pp. 214-215.

[12] *See* Scott Paltrowitz, Briefing Transcript, p. 264.

[13] Joe Palazzolo, *Racial Gap in Men's Sentencing*, WALL ST. J., Feb. 14, 2013, *available at* http://online.wsj.com/news/articles/SB10001424127887324432004578304463789858002 (last accessed Oct. 21, 2014).

[14] U.S. DEPARTMENT OF JUSTICE, OFFICE OF JUSTICE PROGRAMS, BUREAU OF JUSTICE ASSISTANCE, JUVENILES IN ADULT PRISONS AND JAILS: A NATIONAL ASSESSMENT, p. 5 (2000), *available at* http://www.ncjrs.gov/pdffiles1/bja/182503.pdf (last accessed Oct. 21, 2014).

[15] HUMAN RIGHTS WATCH & THE AMERICAN CIVIL LIBERTIES UNION, GROWING UP LOCKED DOWN: YOUTH IN SOLITARY CONFINEMENT IN JAILS AND PRISONS ACROSS THE UNITED STATES 106 (2012) [hereinafter GROWING UP LOCKED DOWN], *available at* http://www.aclu.org/growinguplockeddown (last accessed Oct. 21, 2014).

[16] *See In re Medley*, 134 U.S. 160, 167-68 (1890) (describing the system of complete isolation in Walnut-Street Penitentiary).

[17] *See* SHARON SHALEV, A SOURCEBOOK ON SOLITARY CONFINEMENT 2 (2008); Craig Haney & Mona Lynch, *Regulating Prisons of the Future: A Psychological Analysis of Supermax and Solitary Confinement*, 23 N.Y.U. REV. L. & SOC. CHANGE 477, 481-82 (1997).

[18] *In re Medley*, 134 U.S. at 168.

[19] *The Use of Solitary Confinement for Juveniles in New York Before the New York State Advisory Committee to the United States Commission on Civil Rights*, at 3 (July 10, 2014) (written statement of Karen L. Murtagh, Executive Director, Prisoners' Legal Services, dated July 10, 2014) [hereinafter Murtagh Written Statement].

[20] *Id.* (citing H. Daniel Butler et al., *Supermax Prisons: Another Chapter in the Constitutionality of the Incarceration Conundrum*, 9 RUTGERS J.L. & PUB. POL'Y, 1, 25 (2012)).

[21] NEW YORK CIVIL LIBERTIES UNION, BOXED IN: THE TRUE COST OF EXTREME ISOLATION IN NEW YORK'S PRISONS 11 (2012) [hereinafter BOXED IN], *available at* http://www.nyclu.org/files/publications/nyclu_boxedin_FINAL.pdf (last accessed Oct. 21, 2014).

[22] JOHN J. GIBBONS & NICHOLAS de B. KATZENBACH, CONFRONTING CONFINEMENT, VERA INSTITUTE OF JUSTICE 52 (2006) [hereinafter CONFRONTING CONFINEMENT], *available at* http://www.vera.org/sites/default/files /resources/downloads/Confronting_Confinement.pdf (last accessed Oct. 21, 2014).

[23] Press Release, Dick Durbin, United States Senator for Illinois and Assistant Majority Leader, Durbin Statement on Federal Bureau of Prisons Assessment of Its Solitary Confinement Practices (Feb. 4, 2014), *available at* http://www.durbin.senate.gov/public/index.cfm /pressreleases?ContentRecord_id=07260483-4972-4720-8d43- 8fc82a9909ac (last accessed Oct. 21, 2014).

[24] CONFRONTING CONFINEMENT at 53.

[25] *Id.* (noting that the growth rate in the numbers of prisoners housed in segregation was 40 percent from 1995-2000 compared with the 28 percent growth rate of the overall prison population).

[26] *The Use of Solitary Confinement for Juveniles in New York Before the New York State Advisory Committee to the United States Commission on Civil Rights*, at 2 (July 10, 2014) (written statement of Ian M. Kysel, Adjunct Professor of Law, Georgetown Law Human Rights Institute, dated July 10, 2014) [hereinafter Kysel Written Statement] (citing DEP'T OF JUSTICE OFFICE OF JUVENILE JUSTICE AND DELINQUENCY PREVENTION, CONDITIONS OF CONFINEMENT: FINDINGS FROM THE SURVEY OF YOUTH IN RESIDENTIAL PLACEMENT 9 (2010), *available at* https://www.ncjrs.gov/pdffiles1/ojjdp /227729.pdf) (last accessed Oct. 21, 2014).

[27] *Id.*

[28] GROWING UP LOCKED DOWN, pp.101-106; Kysel Written Statement, p. 2.

[29] Kysel Written Statement, p. 2.

[30] *Id.* (citing GROWING UP LOCKED DOWN, p. 64).

[31] *Id.* at 1.

[32] Kysel Written Statement, p 5.

[33] *Id.*

[34] *Id.*

[35] Anthony J. Annucci, Briefing Transcript, pp. 73-74.

[36] BOXED IN, at 1.

[37] *Id* at 12.
[38] *Id.* at 13.
[39] *Id.* at 1.
[40] *Id.* at 8.
[41] *Id.* at 9.
[42] *Id.* at 17.
[43] *Id.*
[44] *Id.*
[45] Annucci, Briefing Transcript, p. 75.
[46] Letter from U.S. Dep't of Justice to Mayor Bill DeBlasio 5 (Aug. 4, 2014) [hereinafter DOJ Letter], *available at* http://www.justice.gov/usao/nys/pressreleases/August14/Rikers Report PR/SDNY%20Rikers%20Report.pdf (citing *About DOC*, N.Y.C. DEP'T OF CORRECTION, *available at* http://www.nyc.gov/html/doc/html/about/about_doc.shtml) (last accessed Oct. 21, 2014).
[47] *Id.*
[48] *Id.*
[49] *Id.*
[50] *NYC DOC Facilities Overview*, N.Y.C. DEPARTMENT OF CORRECTION, *available at* http://www.nyc.gov/html/doc/html/about/facilities-overview.shtml.
[51] DOJ Letter, at 5.
[52] *About BOC*, N.Y.C. BOARD OF CORRECTION, *available at* http://www.nyc.gov/html/boc /html/about/about.shtml.
[53] *Id.; see* Bryanne Hamill, Briefing Transcript, pp. 90-93.
[54] DOJ Letter, at 5.
[55] *Id.*
[56] *Id.*
[57] *Id.*
[58] *Id.*
[59] JAMES GILLIGAN & BANDY LEE, REPORT TO THE NEW YORK CITY BOARD OF CORRECTION 2 (2013), [hereinafter Gilligan-Lee Report], *available at* http://solitary watch.com/wp-content/uploads/2013/11/Gilligan-Report.-Final.pdf (last accessed Oct. 21, 2014).
[60] DOJ Letter, at 5.
[61] BOXED IN, at 17.
[62] Karen Murtagh, Briefing Transcript, p. 234.
[63] BOXED IN, at 18.
[64] *Id.*
[65] *Id.* at 18-19.
[66] Murtagh, Briefing Transcript, p. 196.
[67] BOXED IN, at 19.
[68] *Id.* at 20.
[69] *The Use of Solitary Confinement for Juveniles in New York Before the New York State Advisory Committee to the United States Commission on Civil Rights*, at 4 (July 10, 2014) (written statement of The Legal Aid Society) [hereinafter LAS Written Statement] (citing DOJ Letter). Please see the *Peoples* discussion in Chapter 3 regarding limits in solitary confinement for those deemed to have a serious mental illness.
[70] *See* Barbara Hamilton, Briefing Transcript, pp. 222-23.
[71] *Id.* at 223.

[72] Hamill, Briefing Transcript, pp. 114-15.

[73] John Perez, Briefing Transcript, pp. 282-83.

[74] *Id.* at 285.

[75] *Id.* at 286.

[76] *Id.* at 285.

[77] Hamilton, Briefing Transcript, pp. 223-24.

[78] *See* BOXED IN, at 20.

[79] Annucci, Briefing Transcript, pp. 70-73.

[80] BOXED IN, at 20.

[81] BOXED IN, at 21.

[82] Annucci, Briefing Transcript, pp. 119-121.

[83] Stipulation For a Stay With Conditions, *Peoples v. Fischer* (S.D.N.Y. Feb. 19, 2013) (No. 11-cv-2694), available at http://www.nyclu.org/files/releases/Solitary_Stipulation.pdf (last accessed Nov. 6, 2014); Alexander A. Reinert, Briefing Transcript, p. 64

[84] Daniel Dromm, Briefing Transcript, pp. 80-81.

[85] *Id.* at 81.

[86] *Id.*

[87] Hamill, Briefing Transcript, p. 114.

[88] Hamilton, Briefing Transcript, pp. 224-25.

[89] Five Mualimm-Ak, Briefing Transcript, p. 145.

[90] Angela Browne, Briefing Transcript, p. 14.

[91] Hamilton, Briefing Transcript, p. 225.

[92] Mualimm-Ak, Briefing Transcript, p. 137.

[93] *The Use of Solitary Confinement for Juveniles in New York Before the New York State Advisory Committee to the United States Commission on Civil Rights*, at 2 (July 10, 2014) (written statement of the Children's Defense Fund (CDF) – New York, dated Aug. 11, 2014) [hereinafter CDF Written Statement].

[94] *Id.* at 2-3.

[95] Dromm, Briefing Transcript, p. 82.

[96] LAS Written Statement, at 9.

[97] *Id.*

[98] *Id.*

[99] N.Y. Penal Law § 30.00 (establishing 16 years old as the automatic cut-off age for criminal responsibility); *see* ONLY NEW YORK AND NORTH CAROLINA PROSECUTE ALL 16- AND 17-YEAR-OLD CHILDREN AS ADULTS, CITIZENS' COMMITTEE FOR CHILDREN, *available at* http://www.cccnewyork.org/wpcontent/uploads/2013/07/CCC RaisetheAgeFactSheets1.pdf (last accessed Oct. 21, 2014); *see also* LAS Written Statement, at 4; Michael Corriero, Briefing Transcript, pp. 16-20.

[100] N.Y. Penal Law § 30.00; Corriero, Briefing Transcript, pp. 20-21.

[101] *See* CITIZENS CRIME COMMISSION OF NEW YORK CITY, GUIDE TO JUVENILE JUSTICE IN NEW YORK CITY, 19 (2010) [hereinafter GUIDE TO JUVENILE JUSTICE], *available at* http://www.nycrimecommission.org/pdfs/GuideToJuvenileJusticeIn NYC.pdf (last accessed Oct. 21, 2014).

[102] *Id. See* CENTER FOR COURT INNOVATION, THE CRIMINAL JUSTICE RESPONSE TO 16- AND 17-YEAR-OLD DEFENDANTS IN NEW YORK, 1 (June 2014), *available at* http://www.courtinnovation.org/sites/default/files/documents/ADP percent20Y2 percent20 Report percent20_ percent20Final.pdf (last accessed Oct. 21, 2014).

[103] GUIDE TO JUVENILE JUSTICE at 19.

[104] Freeman, Briefing Transcript, p. 219.
[105] *Id.* at 236.
[106] Corriero, Briefing Transcript, p. 17.
[107] *Id.* at 16.
[108] *Id.* at 16-17.
[109] Kysel Written Statement, at 2 (citing GROWING UP LOCKED DOWN, at 131).
[110] *The Use of Solitary Confinement for Juveniles in New York Before the New York State Advisory Committee to the United States Commission on Civil Rights*, at 2 (July 10, 2014) (written statement of Joseph Ponte, Commissioner N.Y.C. Dep't of Correction, dated Aug. 8, 2014) [hereinafter Ponte Written Statement].
[111] N.Y.C. DEP'T OF CORRECTION ANNUAL REPORT FY14 ADOLESCENT, http://www.nyc.gov/html/doc/downloads/pdf/adolescent/census_data/ANNUAL_REPORT_FY14_ADOLESCENT. pdf (last accessed Oct. 21, 2014).
[112] Ponte Written Statement, at 2.
[113] *Id.*
[114] *The Use of Solitary Confinement for Juveniles in New York Before the New York State Advisory Committee to the United States Commission on Civil Rights*, at 2-3 (July 10, 2014) (written statement of Homer D. Venters, MD, MS, Assistant Commissioner Bureau of Correctional Health Services, New York City Department of Health and Mental Hygiene) [hereinafter Venters Written Statement].
[115] Kysel Written Statement, at 2.
[116] Benjamin Weiser, *New York State in Deal to Limit Solitary Confinement*, N.Y. TIMES, Feb. 19, 2014, *available at* http://www.nytimes.com/2014/02/20/nyregion/new-york-state-agrees-to-big-changes-in-how-prisons-disciplineinmates.html (last accessed Oct. 21, 2014).
[117] Dromm, Briefing Transcript, p. 83.
[118] Kysel Written Statement, at 2 (citing *Growing Up Locked Down* at 131).
[119] Ponte Written Statement, at 3.
[120] *Id.* (citing Benjamin Weiser, *New York State in Deal to Limit Solitary Confinement*, N.Y. TIMES, Feb. 19, 2014, *available at* http://www.nytimes.com/2014/02/20/nyregion/new-york-state-agrees-to-big-changes-in-how-prisonsdiscipline-inmates.html (last accessed Oct. 21, 2014).
[121] Kysel Written Statement, at 2.
[122] Corriero, Briefing Transcript, p. 61.
[123] Paltrowitz, Briefing Transcript, p. 258.
[124] *Id.* at 308.
[125] DOJ Letter, at 49.
[126] *Id.*
[127] *Id.*
[128] Murtagh, Briefing Transcript, p. 199.
[129] *Id.* at 200.
[130] Hamilton, Briefing Transcript, p. 223.
[131] *Id.*
[132] *Id.* at 223-24.
[133] *Id.* at 224.
[134] Jennifer Parish, Briefing Transcript, p. 209.
[135] Freeman, Briefing Transcript, p. 219.
[136] DOJ Letter, at 9.
[137] *Id.* at 7.

[138] *Id.* at 8.
[139] *Id.*
[140] *Id.*
[141] Paltrowitz, Briefing Transcript, p. 259.
[142] *Id.*
[143] *Id.* at 260.
[144] Mualimm-Ak, Briefing Transcript, p. 142.
[145] CDF Written Statement, at 5.
[146] *Id.* at 5; *see also* Corriero, Briefing Transcript, p.18.
[147] CDF Written Statement, at 5.
[148] Corriero, Briefing Transcript, p. 18.
[149] BOXED IN, at 24.
[150] *Id.*
[151] *Id.* at 23.
[152] DOJ Letter, at 48.
[153] *Id.*
[154] Dromm, Briefing Transcript, pp. 84, 124.
[155] DOJ Letter, at 48.
[156] *Id.*
[157] BOXED IN, at 27.
[158] Murtagh Written Statement, at 6.
[159] Annucci, Briefing Transcript, pp. 76-77.
[160] BOXED IN, at 27.
[161] Kysel Written Statement, at 1.
[162] Reinert, Briefing Transcript, p. 55.
[163] *Id.*
[164] BOXED IN, at 27.
[165] DOJ Letter, at 47.
[166] BOXED IN, at 32.
[167] *Id.* at 28.
[168] *Id.*
[169] N.Y. COMP. CODES R. & REGS. tit. 7, § 305.2(a) (2014).
[170] BOXED IN, at 37-38.
[171] *Id.* at 37.
[172] *Id. See* Murtagh, Briefing Transcript, pp. 244-45.
[173] *Id.*
[174] *Id.* at 245.
[175] BOXED IN, at 35.
[176] *Id.*
[177] Hamilton, Briefing Transcript, p. 221.
[178] DOJ Letter, at 47.
[179] *Id.*
[180] *Id.*
[181] DOJ Letter, at 47.
[182] *Id.*
[183] N.Y.C. BOARD OF CORRECTION, BARRIERS TO RECREATION AT RIKERS ISLAND'S CENTRAL PUNITIVE SEGREGATION UNIT (2014) at 3 [hereinafter

BARRIERS TO RECREATION], *available at* http://www.nyc.gov/html/boc/downloads/pdf/reports/CPSU_Rec_Report.pdf (last accessed Oct. 21, 2014).

[184] *Id.* at 9.

[185] *Id.* at 10.

[186] *Id.* at 10-12.

[187] *See generally id.*; DOJ Letter, at 47.

[188] N.Y.C. BOARD OF CORRECTION, STAFF REPORT: THREE ADOLESCENTS WITH MENTAL ILLNESS IN PUNITIVE SEGREGATION AT RIKERS ISLAND (2013) [hereinafter THREE ADOLESCENTS], *available at* http://www.nyc.gov/html/boc/downloads/pdf/reports/Three_Adolescents_BOC_staff_report.pdf (last accessed Oct. 21, 2014).

[189] *Id.*

[190] *Id. See* Dromm, Briefing Transcript, p. 84.

[191] *Id.*

[192] LAS Written Statement, at 10.

[193] Dromm, Briefing Transcript, p. 84.

[194] *Id.*

[195] LAS Written Statement, at 5. As Judge Corriero quoted from the Office of Children and Family Services' rules and regulations during the briefing, "Room confinement of children shall not be used for punishment. It should be authorized only in cases where a child constitutes a serious and evident danger to himself, herself or others, but once that child turns 16 they go into the adult system, they're viewed through the lens of prosecuting children as adults." Corriero, Briefing Transcript, p. 19.

[196] Freeman, Briefing Transcript, p. 218.

[197] *See* LAS Written Statement, at 5.

[198] Parish, Briefing Transcript, pp. 205-06.

[199] *Id.* at 206.

[200] *Id.* at 206-07.

[201] *Id.* at 207-09.

[202] *Id.*

[203] *Id.* at 209.

[204] *Id.*

[205] DOJ Letter, at 50.

[206] *Id.*

[207] *Id.*

[208] *Id.*

[209] *Id.*

[210] *Id.*

[211] Venters Written Statement, at 4.

[212] *Id.*

[213] *Id.*

[214] *Id.*

[215] *Id.*

[216] Hamill, Briefing Transcript, pp. 117-18.

[217] *Id.*

[218] Press Release, New York Campaign for Alternatives to Isolated Confinement, Lawmakers, Advocates, and Survivors of Solitary Confinement Introduce Sweeping Reforms to Use of Isolation in New York's Prisons and Jails (May 5, 2014), *available at* http://nycaic.org

/2014/05/05/news-lawmakers-advocates-and-survivors-of-solitaryconfinement-introduce-sweeping-reforms-to-use-of-isolation-in-new-yorks-prisons-and-jails/.

[219] *Id.*

[220] Stipulation For a Stay With Conditions, *Peoples* v. *Fischer*, at 3 (S.D.N.Y. filed Feb. 19, 2013) (11-cv-2694) *available at* http://www.nyclu.org/files/releases/Solitary_Stipulation.pdf (last accessed Nov. 7, 2014).

[221] Press Release, New York Governor Andrew Cuomo, Governor Cuomo Announces Members of Comm'n on Youth, Public Safety & Justice (Apr. 9, 2014), *available at* https://www.governor.ny.gov/press/04092014- commission-ypsj.

[222] *Id.*

[223] Michael Schwirtz, *Law Boosts Oversight of Use of Solitary Confinement at Rikers Island*, N.Y. TIMES, Aug. 28, 2014, *available at* http://www.nytimes.com/2014/08/29/nyregion/new-law-boosts-oversight-of-use-of-solitaryconfinement-at-rikers.html?_r=0.

[224] Michael Schwirtz, *Solitary Confinement to End for Youngest at Rikers Island*, N.Y. TIMES, Sept. 28, 2014, *available at* http://www.nytimes.com/2014/09/29/nyregion/solitary-confinement-to-end-for-youngest-at-rikersisland.html.

[225] *Id.*

[226] *Id.*

[227] City of New York, Mayor Bill de Blasio, Mayor's Task Force on Behavioral Health and the Criminal Justice System, Action Plan, Dec. 1, 2014.

[228] *Id.* at 12.

[229] *Id.*

[230] Kysel Written Statement, at 4.

[231] *Id.*

[232] Juvenile Justice Reform Committee, *Solitary Confinement of Juvenile Offenders*, AM. ACAD. CHILD & ADOLESCENT PSYCHIATRY (Apr. 2012), *available at* http://www.aacap.org/aacap/Policy_Statements/2012/Solitary_Confinement_of_Juvenile_Offenders.aspx.

[233] Kysel Written Statement, at 3.

[234] *See* GROWING UP LOCKED DOWN, at 23.

[235] *Id.*

[236] Lee, Briefing Transcript, p. 159.

[237] *Id.* at 159-60.

[238] *Id.* at 162.

[239] *See* Kysel Written Statement, at 6 (citing *Roper* v. *Simmons*, 453 U.S. 551 (2005), *Miller* v. *Alabama*, 132 S. Ct. 2455 (2012), *Graham* v. *Florida*, 560 U.S. 48 (2010), and *J.D.B.* v. *North Carolina*, 131 S. Ct. 2394 (2011)).

[240] Murtagh, Briefing Transcript, p. 192.

[241] *See id.*

[242] JONATHAN LIPPMAN, THE STATE OF THE JUDICIARY 2013, at 9, *available at* http://www.nycourts.gov/ctapps/news/SOJ-2013.pdf (last accessed Oct. 21, 2014).

[243] Letter from Robert L. Listenbee, Adm'r, U.S. Dep't of Justice, Office of Juvenile Justice and Delinquency Prevention to Jesselyn McCurdy, Senior Legislative Counsel, Am. Civil Liberties Union 1 (July 5, 2013), *available at* https://www.aclu.org/sites/default/files/assets/doj_ojjdp_response_on_jj_solitary.pdf (last accessed Oct. 21, 2014).

[244] Lee, Briefing Transcript, p. 162.

[245] GROWING UP LOCKED DOWN, at 15.

[246] Kysel Written Statement, at 4.

[247] *Id.*

[248] GROWING UP LOCKED DOWN, at 15 (citing Jay N. Giedd, *Structural Magnetic Resonance Imaging of the Adolescent Brain*, 1021 ANNALS N.Y. ACAD. SCI. 77, 83 (2004)).

[249] *Id.* at 16.

[250] Venters Written Statement, at 2.

[251] *See* Freeman, Briefing Transcript, p. 216; Lee, Briefing Transcript, p. 158; Murtagh, Briefing Transcript, p. 193.

[252] Paltrowitz, Briefing Transcript, p. 262.

[253] *Id.* at 267-68.

[254] *See* Lee, Briefing Transcript, p. 158.

[255] *Id.* at 159.

[256] *Id.* at 184.

[257] *Id.*

[258] Fatos Kaba, M.A., et al., *Traumatic Brain Injury Among Newly Admitted Adolescents in the New York City Jail System*, 54 J. Adolescent Health 615 (2012).

[259] Jake Peterson, *Nearly Half of All Jailed Youths In New York City Have Brain Injury*, THE HUFFINGTON POST, Apr. 18, 2014, *available at* http://www.huffingtonpost.com /2014/04/18/study-half-of-jailed-nyc_n_5175209.html (last accessed Oct. 21, 2014). John D. Corrigan, professor in the Department of Physical Medicine and Rehabilitation at the Ohio State University stated "[w]hat's happening with many of these kids, these young adults in the criminal population, is they're having them early in life" but the consequences are not noticed until later. I*d.*

[260] GROWING UP LOCKED DOWN, at 132.

[261] Lee, Briefing Transcript, p. 160.

[262] CDF Written Statement, at 3 (citing JAMES GILLIGAN & BANDY LEE., REPORT TO THE NEW YORK CITY BOARD OF CORRECTION at 2 (2013), [hereinafter Gilligan-Lee Report], *available at* http://solitarywatch.com/wp-content/uploads/2013/11/Gilligan-Report.-Final.pdf (last accessed Oct. 21, 2014).

[263] *Id.* at 2.

[264] Gilligan-Lee Report, at 2.

[265] *Id.* at 3.

[266] GROWING UP LOCKED DOWN, at 24.

[267] Murtagh, Briefing Transcript, p. 193.

[268] Kysel Written Statement, at 3.

[269] *Id.* (citing GROWING UP LOCKED DOWN, at 25).

[270] *Id.* (citing GROWING UP LOCKED DOWN, at 33).

[271] *Id.* (citing GROWING UP LOCKED DOWN, at 33).

[272] Dromm, Briefing Transcript, pp. 81-82.

[273] Murtagh, Briefing Transcript, p. 199.

[274] *Id.* at 200.

[275] Dromm, Briefing Transcript, pp. 81-82.

[276] Kysel Written Statement, at 3 (citing GROWING UP LOCKED DOWN, at 27).

[277] *Id.*, at 3 (citing GROWING UP LOCKED DOWN, at 34).

[278] *Id.*

[279] *Id.*

[280] *Id.* (citing LINDSAY M. HAYES, DEP'T OF JUSTICE OFFICE OF JUVENILE JUSTICE AND DELINQUENCY PREVENTION, JUVENILE SUICIDES IN CONFINEMENT: A NATIONAL SURVEY (2009), *available at* https://www.ncjrs.gov/pdffiles1/ojjdp

/213691.pdf (last accessed Oct. 21, 2014); CHRISTOPHER MUOLA, U.S. DEP'T OF JUSTICE, BUREAU OF JUSTICE STATISTICS, SUICIDE AND HOMICIDE IN STATE PRISONS AND LOCAL JAILS (2005), *available at* http://bjs.ojp.usdoj.gov/content/pub/pdf/shsplj.pdf (last accessed Oct. 21, 2014); Seena Fazel et al., *Suicide in Prisoners: A Systematic Review of Risk Factors*, 69 J. CLIN. PSYCHIATRY 1721 (2008), *available at* http://www.ncbi.nlm.nih.gov/pubmed/19026254 (last accessed Oct. 21, 2014); Homer Venters et al., Solitary Confinement and Risk of Self-Harm Among Jail Inmates, 104 AM. J. PUB. HEALTH 442 (2014), *available at* http://ajph.aphapublications.org/doi/full/10.2105/AJPH.2013.301742 (last accessed Oct. 21, 2014)).

[281] *Id.*

[282] Hamilton, Briefing Transcript, p. 227.

[283] *Id.*

[284] *Id.*

[285] *Id.*

[286] *Id.* at 227-28.

[287] Mualimm-Ak, Briefing Transcript, pp. 141-42.

[288] Perez, Briefing Transcript, p. 284.

[289] Megan Crowe-Rothstein, Briefing Transcript, p. 167.

[290] *Id.* at 168.

[291] *Id.*

[292] *Id.*

[293] Lee, Briefing Transcript, pp. 160-61 (Bandy Lee).

[294] Gilligan-Lee Report, at 9.

[295] *Id.*

[296] Murtagh, Briefing Transcript, p. 201.

[297] *Id.*

[298] *Id.*

[299] Crowe-Rothstein, Briefing Transcript, p. 169.

[300] *Id.* at 169-70.

[301] Kysel Written Statement, at 3.

[302] *Id.*

[303] *Id.* at 4.

[304] Lee, Briefing Transcript, p. 163.

[305] Kysel Written Statement, at 4.

[306] Lee, Briefing Transcript, p. 159.

[307] Kysel Written Statement, at 4.

[308] *Id.*

[309] *Id.*

[310] Dromm, Briefing Transcript, p. 83.

[311] Hamill, Briefing Transcript, p. 98.

[312] 20 U.S.C. §§ 1400 *et seq.* (2012).

[313] Kysel Written Statement, at 5.

[314] *Id.* at 4.

[315] Dromm, Briefing Transcript, p. 128.

[316] *Educational and Vocational Programs in Prison Before the State of New York Dep't of Corr. and Community Supervision* at 1 (Nov. 29, 2012) (statement of Commissioner Brian Fischer), *available at* http://www.doccs.ny.gov/Commissioner/Testimony/Educational_Vocational_Programs.pdf [hereinafter DOCCS Hearing] at 1 (last accessed Oct. 21, 2014).

[317] *Id.* at 2.
[318] *Id.*
[319] Ponte Written Statement, at 2.
[320] Children's Defense Fund Written Statement, at 4. *See also* DOJ Letter, at 47; Dromm, Briefing Transcript, p. 127.
[321] Children's Defense Fund Written Statement, at 4.
[322] Kysel Written Statement, at 4.
[323] Freeman, Briefing Transcript, p. 219.
[324] *Id.* at 219-20.
[325] Marybeth Zeman, Briefing Transcript, p. 276.
[326] Perez, Briefing Transcript, p. 287.
[327] Zeman, Briefing Transcript, p. 278.
[328] Browne, Briefing Transcript, p. 12.
[329] Dromm, Briefing Transcript, p. 85.
[330] *Id.*
[331] *Id.*
[332] Annucci, Briefing Transcript, p. 85.
[333] Kysel Written Statement, at 6.
[334] *Id.* (citing *Roper* v. *Simmons*, 453 U.S. 551 (2005), *Miller* v. *Alabama*, 132 S. Ct. 2455 (2012), *Graham* v. *Florida*, 560 U.S. 48 (2010), and *J.D.B.* v. *North Carolina*, 131 S.Ct. 2394 (2011)).
[335] *Id.* at 4.
[336] U.S. CONST. Amend. V; U.S. CONST. Amend. XIV, § 1; U.S. CONST. Amend VIII. *See also* Kysel Written Statement, at 6 (citing *Schall* v. *Martin*, 467 U.S. 253, 269 (1984); *Morgan* v. *Sproat*, 432 F. Supp. 1130, 1135 (S.D. Miss. 1977)) (noting that "some courts apply both the Substantive Due Process protections as well as the prohibition against Cruel and Unusual punishment to conditions claims of post-adjudication youth.").
[337] Kysel Written Statement, at 6 (citing *Cnty. of Sacramento* v. *Lewis*, 523 U.S. 833, 846 (1998)).
[338] *Id.* at 7.
[339] *See The Use of Solitary Confinement for Juveniles in New York Before the New York State Advisory Committee to the United States Commission on Civil Rights*, at 3 (July 10, 2014) (written statement of Alexander A. Reinert) [hereinafter Reinert Written Statement] (quoting *Smith* v. *Coughlin*, 748 F.2d 783, 787 (2d Cir. 1984) (internal quotations omitted)).
[340] Reinert Written Statement, at 3 (quoting *Trop* v. *Dulles*, 356 U.S. 86, 100-01 (1958)).
[341] *Farmer* v. *Brennan*, 511 U.S. 825, 832 (1994) (quoting *Hudson* v. *Palmer*, 468 U.S. 517, 526-27 (1984)).
[342] Kysel Written Statement, at 6.
[343] *Id.* at 5 (citing *D.B.* v. *Tewksbury*, 545 F. Supp. 896, 905 (D. Or. 1982); *Lollis* v. *N.Y. State Dep't of Soc. Servs.*, 322 F. Supp. 473, 480-82 (S.D.N.Y. 1970)).
[344] *Lollis*, 322 F. Supp. at 482.
[345] *Id.* at 481-82.
[346] *Inmates of Boys' Training School* v. *Affleck*, 346 F. Supp. 1354, 1366 (D.R.I. 1972).
[347] *Id.* at 1366.
[348] *R.G.* v. *Koller*, 415 F. Supp. 2d 1129, 1155-56 (D. Haw. 2006).
[349] Kysel Written Statement, at 6 (collecting cases).
[350] Reinert Written Statement, at 4 (citing *In re Medley*, 143 U.S. 160, 168 (1890)).
[351] *Id.* at 5.

[352] 42 U.S.C. § 1983, which provides individuals the power to bring a civil action against state actors for any deprivation of rights, privileges, or immunities under the Constitution.

[353] 545 U.S. 209 (2005).

[354] *Id.* at 214.

[355] Reinert Written Statement, at 5-6.

[356] Kysel Written Statement, at 5.

[357] *Id.* (citing Consent Decree, C.B., et al. v. Walnut Grove Corr. Facility, No. 3:10-cv-663 (S.D. Miss. 2012) (prohibiting solitary confinement of children); Settlement Agreement, Raistlen Katka v. Montana State Prison, No. BDV 2009-1163 (Apr. 12, 2012), available at http://www.aclumontana.org/images/stories/documents/litigation/katkasettlement.pdf (limiting the use of isolation and requiring special permission); Benjamin Weiser, *New York State in Deal to Limit Solitary Confinement*, N.Y. TIMES, Feb. 19, 2014, *available at* http://www.nytimes.com/2014/02/20/nyregion/new-york-state-agrees-to-bigchanges-in-how-prisons-discipline-inmates.html?r=0).

[358] *Id.* (citing PERFORMANCE-BASED STANDARDS, REDUCING ISOLATION AND ROOM CONFINEMENT 4 (Sept. 2012), *available at* http://pbstandards.org/uploads /documents/PbS_Reducing_Isolation_Room_Confinement_201209.pdf (last accessed Oct. 21, 2014).

[359] *Id.* (stating "These states at a minimum either ban punitive solitary confinement or heavily restrict its use. . ." and citing Alaska Delinquency Rule 13 (Oct. 15, 2012) ("a juvenile may not be confined in solitary confinement for punitive reasons."); Conn. Gen. Stat. Ann. § 46b-133 (2012) ("No child shall at any time be held in solitary confinement[.]"); Me. Rev. Stat. tit. 34-A § 3032 (5) (2006) (including "segregation" in the list of punishments for adults, but not in the list for children); Nev. Rev. Stat. § 62B (2013) ("a child who is detained in a local or regional facility for the detention of children may be subjected to corrective room restriction only if all other less-restrictive options have been exhausted and only [for listed purposes]."); Okla. Admin. Code § 377:35-11-4 (2013) ("solitary confinement is a serious and extreme measure to be imposed only in emergency situations[.]"); W. Va. Code § 49-5- 16a (1998) ("A juvenile may not be punished by . . . imposition of solitary confinement and except for sleeping hours, a juvenile in a state facility may not be locked alone in a room unless that juvenile is not amenable to reasonable direction and control.").

[360] Reinert Written Statement, at 6.

[361] *Id.*

[362] *Id.*

[363] *Id.*

[364] *Id.*

[365] *Id.* at 7.

[366] *Id.*

[367] *Id.*

[368] *Id.*

[369] *Id.*

[370] *Id.* at 7-8.

[371] *Id.* at 6.

[372] *Id.* at 8.

[373] Kysel Written Statement, at 5.

[374] *Id.*

[375] *See* Freeman, Briefing Transcript, p. 236.

[376] Youthful Inmates, 28 C.F.R. § 115.14 (2012).

[377] *Id.*

[378] Kysel Written Statement, at 5.

[379] *See* Youthful Inmates, 28 C.F.R. § 115.51(a) ("agency shall provide multiple internal ways for inmates to privately report sexual abuse and sexual harassment, retaliation by other inmates or staff for reporting sexual abuse and sexual harassment, and staff neglect or violation of responsibilities that may have contributed to such incidents"); *Id.* at §115.51(b) ("[t]he agency shall also provide at least one way for inmates to report abuse or harassment to a public or private entity or office that is not part of the agency, and that is able to receive and immediately forward inmate reports of sexual abuse and sexual harassment to agency officials, allowing the inmate to remain anonymous upon request."); *Id.* at § 115.67(a) ("[t]he agency shall establish a policy to protect all inmates and staff who report sexual abuse or sexual harassment or cooperate with sexual abuse or sexual harassment investigations from retaliation by other inmates or staff, and shall designate which staff members or departments are charged with monitoring retaliation"); §115.71(e) ("[t]he credibility of an alleged victim, suspect, or witness shall be assessed on an individual basis and shall not be determined by the person's status as inmate or staff").

[380] 42 U.S.C. § 1997 (1980).

[381] *Id.* § 1997a(a).

[382] CDF Written Statement, at 2.

[383] 42 U.S.C. § 14141(a) (1994).

[384] *Id.* § 14141(b).

[385] Kysel Written Statement, at 7.

[386] *Trop* v. *Dulles*, 356 U.S. 86, 101 (1958).

[387] Kysel Written Statement, at 7.

[388] *Id.* at 6.

[389] International Covenant on Civil and Political Rights arts. 10, 14(4), *opened for signature* Dec. 16, 1966, S. Exec. Rep. 102-23, 999 U.N.T.S. 171 (entered into force Mar. 23, 1976), *available at* http://www.ohchr.org/en/professionalinterest/pages/ccpr.aspx (last accessed Oct. 21, 2014).

[390] Comm. on the Rights of the Child, Rep. on its 44th Sess. (Jan. 15-Feb. 2, 2007), U.N. Doc. CRC/C/GC/10 (Apr. 25, 2007), *available at* http://www1.umn.edu/humanrts/crc/comment10.html (last accessed Oct. 21, 2014); U.N. Rules for the Protection of Juveniles Deprived of Their Liberty, G.A. Res. 45/113, Annex, U.N. GAOR, 45th Sess., Supp. No. 49A, U.N. Doc. A/45/49, ¶ 67 (Dec. 14, 1990) ("The Beijing Rules"), *available at* http://www.unrol.org/doc.aspx?d=2554 (last accessed Oct. 21, 2014).

[391] Press Release, Annex to the Press Release Issued at the Close of the 147th Session (Apr. 5, 2013), *available at* http://www.oas.org/en/iachr/media_center/PReleases/2013/023A.asp (incorporating the definition of the United Nations Special Rapporteur on Torture, Mr. Juan Mendez, into the IACHR corpus juris) (last accessed Oct. 21, 2014).

[392] Kysel Written Statement, at 6.

[393] S. 2567, 113th Cong. (2014).

[394] *See id.*

[395] Press Release, Cory Booker, United States Senator for New Jersey, U.S. Senators Booker and Paul Introduce Legislation Calling for Criminal Justice Reform (July 8, 2014), *available at* http://www.booker.senate.gov/?p=press_release&id=100.

[396] *Id.*

[397] *Id.*

[398] Reinert Written Statement, at 2.
[399] *Id.*
[400] Hamilton, Briefing Transcript, pp. 221-22.
[401] Murtagh, Briefing Transcript, p. 246.
[402] Freeman, Briefing Transcript, p. 246.
[403] Murtagh, Briefing Transcript, p. 249.
[404] Michael Schwirtz, *Law Boosts Oversight of Use of Solitary Confinement*, N.Y.TIMES, Aug. 29, 2014, *available at* http://www.nytimes.com/2014/08/29/nyregion/new-law-boosts-oversight-of-use-of-solitary-confinement-atrikers.html (last accessed Oct. 21, 2014).
[405] *Id.*
[406] Hamill, Briefing Transcript, pp. 90-93.
[407] *Id.* at 90.
[408] *Id.* at 98-99.
[409] City of New York, Mayor Bill de Blasio, Mayor's Task Force on Behavioral Health and the Criminal Justice System, Action Plan, Dec. 1, 2014.
[410] *Id.* at 12.
[411] *Id.*
[412] *Id.*
[413] *Id.*
[414] *Id.*
[415] *Id.*
[416] *Id.*
[417] Press Release, New York Campaign for Alternatives to Isolated Confinement, Lawmakers, Advocates, and Survivors of Solitary Confinement Introduce Sweeping Reforms to Use of Isolation in New York's Prisons and Jails (May 5, 2014), *available at* http://nycaic.org/2014/05/05/news-lawmakers-advocates-and-survivors-of-solitary-confinement-introduce-sweeping-reforms-to-use-of-isolation-in-new-yorks-prisons-and-jails.
[418] *Id.*
[419] *Id.*
[420] *Id.*
[421] *Id.*
[422] Governor Cuomo Announces Members of Commission on Youth, Public Safety & Justice, *available at* https://www.governor.ny.gov/press/04092014-commission-ypsj (last accessed Oct. 21, 2014).
[423] *Id.*
[424] *Id.*
[425] Stipulation For a Stay With Conditions, *Peoples* v. *Fischer*, at 3 (S.D.N.Y. filed Feb. 19, 2013) (11-cv-2694), *available at* http://www.nyclu.org/files/releases/Solitary_Stipulation.pdf (last accessed Nov. 6, 2014) .
[426] *Peoples* v. *Fischer*, No. 11-cv-2694 (S.D.N.Y. Apr. 18, 2011).
[427] Third Amended Class Action Complaint, at 1-6, *Peoples* v. *Fischer* (S.D.N.Y. Mar. 5, 2013) (No. 11-cv-2694).
[428] *Id.* at 2.
[429] Stipulation For a Stay With Conditions, *Peoples* v. *Fischer* (S.D.N.Y. Feb. 19, 2013) (No. 11-cv-2694), *available at* http://www.nyclu.org/files/releases/Solitary_Stipulation.pdf (last accessed Nov. 6, 2014) .
[430] *Id.* at 3.

[431] *Id.*

[432] *Id.*

[433] Reinert, Briefing Transcript, p. 42.

[434] *Id.* at 43.

[435] Stipulation For a Stay With Conditions at 5, *Peoples* v. *Fischer* (S.D.N.Y. Feb. 19, 2013) (No. 11-cv-2694), *available at* http://www.nyclu.org/files/releases/Solitary_Stipulation.pdf (last accessed Nov. 6, 2014).

[436] Reinert Written Statement, at 15.

[437] Murtagh, Briefing Transcript, p. 198.

[438] *Id.*

[439] *Id.* at 199.

[440] Kysel Written Statement, at 5.

[441] Press Release, U.S. Dep't of Justice, Attorney General Holder Criticizes Excessive Use of Solitary Confinement for Juveniles with Mental Illness (May 14, 2014), *available at* http://www.justice.gov/opa/pr/attorney-generalholder-criticizes-excessive-use-solitary-confinement-juveniles-mental (last accessed Oct. 21, 2014).

[442] Kysel Written Statement, at 5.

[443] Letter from Thomas E. Perez, Assistant Attorney Gen., U.S. Dep't of Justice, to The Honorable Andrew J. Spano, County Executive 40-41 (Nov. 19, 2009), *available at* http://www.justice.gov/crt/about/spl/documents/Westchester_findlet_11-19-09.pdf (last accessed Oct. 21, 2014).

[444] *Case Summaries: United States* v. *Erie County, New York, No. 1:09-cv-00849 (W.D.N.Y.), Buffalo, NY*, U.S. DEP'T JUST., *available at* http://www.justice.gov/crt/about/spl/case summaries.php#erie-summ (last visited Oct. 8, 2014).

[445] DOJ Letter, at 3.

[446] NATIONAL RESEARCH COUNCIL OF THE ACADEMIES, REFORMING JUVENILE JUSTICE: A DEVELOPMENTAL APPROACH (2013), *available at* http://www.colorado.gov/ccjjdir/Resources/Resources/Ref/ReformingJJDevApproach-2013.pdf (last accessed Oct. 21, 2014).

[447] NATIONAL RESEARCH COUNCIL OF THE NATIONAL ACADEMIES, IMPLEMENTING JUVENILE JUSTICE REFORM: THE FEDERAL ROLE at vii (2014), *prepublication available at* http://www.njjn.org/uploads/digital-library/ImplementingJJ-Reform-federal-Role_September-2014.pdf (last accessed Oct. 21, 2014).

[448] Press Release, Dick Durbin, United States Senator for Illinois and Assistant Majority Leader, Durbin Statement on Federal Bureau of Prisons Assessment of Its Solitary Confinement Practices (Feb. 4, 2013), *available at* http://www.durbin.senate.gov/public/index.cfm /pressreleases?ContentRecord_id=07260483-4972-4720-8d43- 8fc82a9909ac.

[449] *Id.*

[450] *Reassessing Solitary Confinement II: The Human Rights, Fiscal, and Public Safety Consequences Before the S. Judiciary Subcomm. on the Constitution, Civil Rights, and Human Rights*, 113th Cong. (2014), *available at* http://www.judiciary.senate.gov/meetings /reassessing-solitary-confinement-ii-the-human-rights-fiscal-and-publicsafety-consequences (last accessed Nov. 10, 2014).

[451] Press Release, Dick Durbin, United States Senator for Illinois and Assistant Majority Leader, Durbin: Time to End Use of Solitary Confinement for Juveniles, Pregnant Women, and those with Serious Mental Illness (Feb. 25, 2014), *available at* http://www.durbin.senate.gov/public/index.cfm/pressreleases?ID=c684591f-9197-4306-8af0- f99141117f287.

[452] LAS Written Statement, at 9.

[453] *Id.*
[454] *Id.*
[455] *Id.* at 11.
[456] *Id.*
[457] *Id.* at 14.
[458] *Id.*
[459] Murtagh, Briefing Transcript, p. 241.
[460] *Id.* at 242.
[461] LAS Written Statement, at 11.
[462] *Id.*
[463] *Id.* at 13.
[464] Paltrowitz, Briefing Transcript, p. 266.
[465] *Id.* at 267.
[466] N.Y STATE BAR ASS'N, COMM. ON CIVIL RIGHTS, SOLITARY CONFINEMENT IN NEW YORK STATE at 2 (2013), *available at* http://www.nysba.org/WorkArea/DownloadAsset.aspx?id=26699 (last accessed Oct. 21, 2014).
[467] *Id.* at 1.
[468] PREA Standard, 28 C.F.R. § 115.51(b) (2012).
[469] PREA Standard 28 C.F.R. §115.71(e) (2012).
[470] *See* PREA Standard, 28 C.F.R. § 115.71(c) ("[i]nvestigators ... shall review prior complaints and reports of sexual abuse involving the suspected perpetrator").

In: Youth in Solitary Confinement
Editor: Meghan Lloyd
ISBN: 978-1-63483-530-5


*Chapter 2*

# TESTIMONY OF PIPER KERMAN, AUTHOR. HEARING ON "REASSESSING SOLITARY CONFINEMENT II: THE HUMAN RIGHTS, FISCAL AND PUBLIC SAFETY CONSEQUENCES"*

Chairman Durbin, Ranking Member Cruz, and distinguished members of the Subcommittee, I want to thank you all for this opportunity to address you and for organizing this important hearing.

I spent 13 months as a prisoner in the Federal Bureau of Prisons system from 2004- 2005, with most of my time served at the Federal Correctional Institution in Danbury, Connecticut. From my first hours of incarceration, whispers and warnings about solitary confinement – better known as the SHU – came with frequency and from all quarters, prisoners and staff alike. One of the first women to befriend me in prison had just spent a month in the SHU for a minor infraction. Solitary confinement is a prison within a prison. But unlike the hive-like communities of people that exist behind prison walls, which have conflicts but also opportunities for redemption, 24-hour lockdown leaves you completely alone in a six-by-eight foot cell for weeks, sometimes months and even years. Here, the terror and the lasting damage of incarceration may be increased a thousand fold. This is unproductive for individuals, the institutions

* This is an edited, reformatted and augmented version of testimony presented February 25, 2014 before the Senate Judiciary Committee, Subcommittee on the Constitution, Civil Rights and Human Rights.

and the outside communities, to which the vast majority of prisoners will return.

If you are familiar with my book, *Orange is the New Black*, you know I'm the first to acknowledge that unlike many prisoners, I have the resources and support to take my own experiences in prison and use them to try to make critical improvements to this country's criminal justice system. Since my release, I have worked with many criminal justice-involved women who need help advocating for the changes they need to be safe and to get back on their feet. I am here today in that capacity.

If you've watched the Netflix original series adapted from my book, you may recall an episode in which the character that is based on me spends time in the SHU. Although today I will share many stories about solitary confinement, I mercifully did not spend any time in solitary. However, the way solitary confinement is handled on the show is an accurate depiction and the silencing effect of the SHU is very real.

## Women in Solitary Confinement

When we think of solitary confinement, most of us don't picture *women* being subjected to this form of extreme punishment. But the truth is that women prisoners are routinely subjected to solitary confinement in jails, prisons and detention centers across the United States.[1] Increasingly, the American public and our leaders are learning about the profound negative psychological impacts of solitary confinement and the excessive number of people held in these conditions, but I want to talk about the unique harms and dangers of subjecting women prisoners to this practice.

Women are the fastest growing population in the criminal justice system and their families and communities are increasingly affected by what happens behind bars. At least 63% of women in prison are there for a nonviolent offense.[2] However, some of the factors that contribute to these women's incarceration can also end up landing them in solitary confinement. Mental health problems are overwhelmingly prevalent in women's prisons and jails, which have a much higher percentage of mentally ill prisoners than in men's facilities.[3] High incidences of sexual and physical assault[4] are a reality for women in prison, jail, and immigration detention centers, both before and during their incarceration.[5] These facts are very important in relation to the use of solitary. It is critical for our criminal justice system to address the unique situation of women in prison—especially those women subjected to the social and sensory deprivation of solitary confinement.

While I was in prison, I saw many women sent to the SHU for minor infractions such as moving around a housing unit during a count, refusing an order from a correctional officer, and possession of low-level contraband like small amounts of cash (which is largely useless in prison) or having women's underwear from the outside rather than prison-issued underwear. All of these infractions drew at least 30 days in solitary. Sometimes women are sent to the SHU immediately upon their arrival in prison because there aren't any open beds. This is especially terrifying if a woman has never been in prison or jail before, which is often the case. Stories about the SHU are rampant – some told directly by the women who experienced solitary first hand, but often passed along from prisoner to prisoner. They all evoke terror and a conviction to keep your head down and report nothing that you see, hear or experience for fear that you may be locked down in isolation.

I have submitted for the record the full written testimony of Jeanne DiMola, who spent one year of her six-year sentence in solitary. She describes with chilling detail the neglect and abuse she endured while in the SHU and the impact the experience of extreme isolation still has on her as she works hard to get her life back on track. Jeanne writes: "When you have no one to talk to inside a grey, dingy cell with its blacked out window, you start talking to yourself, then you think your inner self at least deserves an answer, so I began answering myself. I asked myself what if I got swallowed into this black hole in my cell and just disappeared. I asked myself if it would be better off for my family if this thorn in their side went away for them so they can truly forget me. The best way I can describe being in this small box when life is going on without you is you are dead and the cell is your coffin. Everything goes on without and around you. But you stay the same...stagnant."

## MENTAL ILLNESS

Mental health experts tell us that solitary confinement is psychologically harmful, especially for people with pre-existing mental illness. Serious mental illness can also result from prisoners' experiences in solitary confinement. In studies of prisoners held in solitary confinement for 10 days or longer, people deteriorated rapidly, with elevated levels of depression and anxiety, a higher propensity to suffer from hallucinations and paranoia, and a higher risk of self-harm and suicide.[6] In solitary confinement units, some prisoners can be found sitting in puddles of their own urine, others smeared in their own feces. The sounds of prisoners shrieking in their cells and banging their fists or heads against the walls is nothing out of the ordinary. Extreme and grotesque self-mutilation is also all too common, such as prisoners who have amputated parts of their own bodies or, in one particularly disturbing case, a prisoner who sewed his mouth shut with a makeshift needle and thread from his pillowcase. Others attempt to or succeed in committing suicide. Regular correctional staff is simply not equipped to deal with the medical issues that are so prevalent within solitary confinement units.

Nearly 75% of women in prison are diagnosed with mental illness. The conditions of confinement are especially difficult for mentally ill people, as adherence to prison rules is simply more difficult for them. This leads to destructive and intense cycles of infractions and punishment. Prisoners with mental illness suffer in ways that make their behavior difficult to manage. They often end up in solitary confinement as a result of behavior that is beyond their control. They are essentially punished for their illness.[7] Putting women with mental illness in solitary confinement only exacerbates a pre-existing illness. They often leave prison in far worse shape than when they went in. Women with mental illness will have great difficulty getting back on their feet and returning successfully to the community unless we mandate through all correctional systems that mentally ill women should not be held in solitary confinement, and should instead be appropriately managed with full medical care.

Consider the story of Jan Green. A 50-year-old grandmother and mother of four,[8] Jan was sent to Valencia County Jail in New Mexico on a domestic violence charge that was later dropped.[9] Staff at the jail knew she had mental health issues when she came in, but instead of giving her treatment, they pepper sprayed her for refusing to wear jail-issued clothing, and eventually put her in solitary confinement where she spent nearly two years in an 8-by-7-foot cell with a mattress on the floor for a bed.[10] Because the water in her cell did not work properly, Jan was unable to wash her hands or shower.[11] Not only did her shower head not work, it dripped constantly.[12] The jail refused to give her toilet paper or sanitary napkins for long periods of time to the point where she was forced to wipe herself with paper bags from her sack lunch.[13] When her family picked her up from jail, she was soiled from dried menstrual blood that had accumulated over several months.[14]

Jan's mental health deteriorated from the constant water drips, being deprived of sanitation, and endless hours of isolation to the point that she spiraled into total psychosis and was ultimately deemed incompetent to stand trial.[15] Her daughter's ongoing attempts to get medical care for her mother failed. Not once was she seen by a psychiatrist or medical doctor.[16] After months in solitary, Jan's lack of exercise and the poor hygiene caused her sock to rot into an open wound on her foot. [17] After nearly two years in solitary, the criminal charges against Jan were finally dismissed and she was released from custody.Her daughter[18] describes the mother she used to know as "outgoing and outspoken," but solitary confinement "shattered her as a person."[xix] When asked about Jan Green, the warden responded: "We're just not equipped with dealing with mental health populations," stating that it was an "economic decision not to provide mental health care."[20]

## Physical and Sexual Abuse

The effects of physical and sexual abuse are also worsened by solitary confinement. I have a vivid memory from early in my prison sentence: a woman who had done a lot of time shared a cautionary tale. She told me about a friend of hers who had gone home not long before; her friend had been sexually abused by a correctional officer, and the abuse was discovered. She told me: "They had her in the SHU for months during the investigation. They shot her full of psych drugs – she blew up like a balloon. When they finally let her out, she was a zombie. It took a long time for her to get back to herself. They do not play here."

Fear of being put in solitary as "protective custody" has a chilling effect on women prisoners' willingness to report sexual abuse, which is commonplace and sometimes rampant in prisons, jails, and detention centers. Another long-time prisoner warned me about a specific correctional officer, calling him a predator; her warning came with a reminder – if a woman ever reported him, she would be locked in the SHU. The terrible threat of isolation makes women afraid to report abuse and serves as a powerful disincentive to ask for help or justice.

In addition, solitary confinement itself can compound the impact of past physical and sexual abuse. A majority of women in state prisons across America report being victims of past physical or sexual abuse.[21] In many prisons across this country, women in solitary confinement are watched by male guards during showers, when undressing and when using the toilet. For the majority of women prisoners who have been victimized by men in the past, being watched by male guards during their most private moments can cause acute psychological suffering.[22]

A recent Equal Justice Initiative investigation into sexual abuse at Alabama's Tutwiler Prison for Women found that women who report sexual abuse, "are routinely placed in segregation by the warden."[23] In the notorious Otter Creek Correctional Center in Kentucky, a woman who saved evidence from her sexual assault (an epidemic problem within the prison with multiple victims) was reportedly placed in segregation for 50 days.[24] At the Dwight Correctional Center in Illinois, a woman alleged in court documents that she was repeatedly raped by prison staff, eventually resulting in a pregnancy and the birth of her son.[25] When the woman tried to report the assaults, she was placed in solitary confinement, and threatened with a longer sentence.[26]

Women who are sexually abused by prison guards are forced to decide between reporting the attack and risking placement in solitary, where they will suffer extreme pain and psychological deterioration, or staying silent and risking further abuse of themselves or others. The use of solitary confinement for "protective custody" perpetuates the cycle of abuse and makes women's prisons more dangerous for the women who live behind their walls.

## IMPACT ON CHILDREN AND FAMILIES

In addition to the damaging effects solitary confinement has on women prisoners, children and families also suffer. Solitary confinement impedes access to important pre-natal and women's health care services. In fact, pregnant women in solitary confinement often receive no medical care.[27] Yet pregnant prisoners in America are still sent to the SHU.

I want to tell you about a female inmate in Illinois who I'll call Meghan out of respect for privacy. She had battled depression for years, and found herself pregnant behind bars. Because of her pregnancy, Meghan had to discontinue some of her mental-health medications. She also needed extra sleep. One day, a guard decided Meghan didn't get up fast enough for mealtime and sent her to solitary confinement as punishment. In solitary, Meghan didn't get her prenatal vitamins. Her requests for water were denied — sometimes for several hours, despite the heat in her isolation cell and the known danger of dehydration during pregnancy. Worse yet, the extreme social isolation in solitary further hampered her fight against clinical depression.

Solitary confinement can also cause lasting damage to families and children. The majority of women in prison were their children's primary or sole caregiver prior to incarceration.[28] When these women are incarcerated, maintaining any semblance of a relationship with their children largely depends on regular visitation.[29] A child's need to see and hold his or her mother is one of the most basic human needs. Yet visitation for prisoners in solitary confinement is extremely limited, with contact visits often forbidden, and often all visitation privileges revoked. This is true even if the infraction is minor, like possession of contraband or disobeying an order. These visitation restrictions mean that, when a mother is held in solitary confinement, her children's visits are either limited to interactions through a physical barrier, such as a glass partition, or eliminated altogether.[30] Through a partition, a child cannot give his or her mother a hug, or hear her voice clearly. The separation is clear. Solitary punishes innocent children.

## CONCLUSION

For many female prisoners, solitary confinement exacerbates the mental health issues and histories of trauma and abuse with which they already struggle. Most women in prison have not committed violent crimes and are not prone to resort to violence while incarcerated. Solitary confinement is an extreme form of punishment, yet its use within women's prisons is routine – sometimes even sinister when it serves to silence women who are being victimized.

We should all share the same goal here: to curb the unnecessary use of solitary confinement in any form. This is possible, and it happens when correctional leaders and staff do the right thing. Last week, I visited the Marion Correctional Institution, a medium security men's state prison in Ohio. It houses a little more than 2,600 men. Since 2011, they have reduced the number of beds at Marion Correctional needed for "administrative segregation" – long-term solitary confinement – by 48 beds, from 175 to 127. They have cut one SHU unit and converted those beds into different, more productive housing. They did this along with an increase in population of approximately 900 men. This change was not the result of a special initiative focused on the SHU. Rather, within the entire institution, the warden and his staff increased prisoners' access to meaningful activities and rehabilitation, to work opportunities, and to incentive-based programs, and in the process they saw solitary confinement numbers come down. This is good for the institution as a whole – prisoners, staff and administration – and proves the point of getting good outcomes in correctional systems: it is always a question of strong leadership and recognition that it is human beings that fill our prisons and jails.

Isolation should only be used when a prisoner is a serious threat to her own safety or that of others; it should never be a long-term solution. When isolation is necessary, the conditions must be humane and rehabilitative. We must ensure that women with mental illness and pregnant women are never subject to solitary. And we must prevent women from being sent to solitary for reporting abuses.

As the Federal Bureau of Prisons pursues an independent assessment of its solitary practices, I urge it to include an assessment of practices at a women's facility, such as the FCIs at Tallahassee, Dublin or Alderson, and take action to limit the use of solitary on women. I ask the assessors to visit as many women's facilities as possible, and to include in the assessment confidential discussions with the women who are incarcerated in those facilities.

I am exceptionally proud to say that last week, my home state of New York announced sweeping reforms of the use of solitary confinement, including the prohibition of placing pregnant women in disciplinary solitary confinement. New York is the first state to agree to this important provision, and the Bureau of Prisons and other states should adopt the same set of sensible comprehensive reforms.

Thank you for the opportunity to participate in this important hearing and to help the Subcommittee address this very significant issue. I am hopeful that it will mark the next step in urgently needed and long-term oversight and reform.

## End Notes

[1] See Joane Martel, Telling the Story: A Study in the Segregation of Women Prisoners, 28 SOC. JUST. 196, 196-197 (2001) (giving an overview of the literature on solitary confinement and finding almost no literature on women in solitary confinement); Cherami Wichmann & Kelly Taylor, Federally Sentenced Women in Administrative Segregation: A Descriptive Analysis (2004) (first quantitative study on segregation of federally sentenced women in Canada). See also infra at 19 and accompanying text.

[2] In 2010, 37% of women in state prison were held for a violent offense, compared with 54% of men. E. ANN CARSON & WILLIAM J. SABOL, BUREAU OF JUST. STAT., PRISONERS IN 2011 9 TBL. 9 (2012), available at http://www.bjs.gov/content/pub/pdf/p11.pdf.

[3] DORIS J. JAMES & LAUREN E. GLAZE, BUREAU OF JUST. STAT., MENTAL HEALTH PROBLEMS OF PRISON AND JAIL INMATES 1 & 4 Tbl. 3 (2006), available at http://www.bjs.gov/content/pub/pdf/mhppji.pdf ("An estimated 73% of females in State prisons, compared to 55% of male[s] had a mental health problem[]. In Federal prisons, the rate was 61% of females compared to 44% of males; and in local jails, 75% of females compared to 63% of male[s].").

[4] In state prison, 57.6% of women reported past physical or sexual abuse, compared to 16.1% of men. In federal prisons, 39.9% of women reported past abuse, compared to 7.2% of men. In jails, 47.6% of women reported past abuse, compared to 12.9% of men. CAROLINE WOLF HARLOW, BUREAU OF JUST. STAT., PRIOR ABUSE REPORTED BY INMATES

AND PROBATIONERS 1 (1999), available at http://www.bjs.gov/content/pub/pdf/parip.pdf. More than a third of women in state prisons or local jails reported being physically or sexually abused before the age of eighteen.

[5] Human Rights Watch, All Too Familiar: Sexual Abuse of Women in U.S. State Prisons (1996), available at http://www.hrw.org/legacy/reports/1996/Us1.htm [hereinafter All Too Familiar] ("One of the clear contributing factors to sexual misconduct in U.S. prisons for women is that the United States, despite authoritative international rules to the contrary, allows male correctional employees to hold contact positions over prisoners, that is, positions in which they serve in constant physical proximity to the prisoners of the opposite sex.").

[6] See Craig Haney, Mental Health Issues in Long-Term Solitary and "Supermax" Confinement, 49 CRIME & DELINQ. 124 (2003); Stanley L. Brodsky & Forrest R. Scogin, Inmates in Protective Custody: First Data on Emotional Effects, 1 FORENSIC REP. 267 (1988); Stuart Grassian, Psychopathological Effects of Solitary Confinement, 140 AM. J. PSYCHOL. 1450 (1983); Holly A. Miller & Glenn R. Young, Prison Segregation: Administrative Detention Remedy or Mental Health Problem?, 7 CRIM. BEHAVIOR & MENTAL HEALTH 85 (1997). See generally HANS TOCH, MOSAIC OF DESPAIR: HUMAN BREAKDOWN IN PRISON (1992).

[7] Id. (describing how some of the women in the California SHU were placed in solitary for behavior that can be a sign of mental health problems).

[8] Compl. at 2, 13, Green v. Chavez, No. 12-CV-1260 MV/KBM, (D. N.M. 2012).

[9] Id. at 3.

[10] Id.

[11] Chris Ramirez, 4 On Your Side Exposes County Jail Shortcomings, EYEWITNESS NEWS 4KOB, Feb. 14, 2014, available at http://www.onenewspage.us/video/20140208/1612385/On-Your-Side-exposes-county-jailshortcomings.htm.

[12] Compl. at 9; Ramirez, supra note 6.

[13] Compl. at 10-11.

[14] Id. at 11; Ramirez, supra note 6.

[15] Id. at 4.

[16] Id. at 3, 7, 15, 17.

[17] Id. at 5.

[18] Id.

[19] Ramirez, supra note 6.

[20] Id.

[21] BUREAU OF JUSTICE STATISTICS, PRIOR ABUSE REPORTED BY INMATES AND PROBATIONERS, supra note 11, at 1; see also LAPIDUS ET AL., CAUGHT IN THE NET, supra note 8, at 47-48 (describing the vulnerabilities of women in prison and in particular the phenomenon of re-traumatization experienced by incarcerated women who have been victims of physical and sexual abuse prior to their incarceration).

[22] See supra note 12 and accompanying text; supra note 49 and accompanying text.

[23] See Equal Justice Initiative, Findings: Equal Justice Initiative Investigation Into Sexual Violence at Tutwiler Prison for Women 2 (May 2012), available at http://www.eji.org/files/EJI%20Findings_from_Tutwiler_Investigation.pdf.

[24] See Kevin Dayton, Incident Leads to Changes at Prison, HONOLULU ADVERTISER, Oct. 2, 2008 (detailing the reports of abuse, and noting that the victim was from Hawai'i); see also Gary Hunter, Sexual Abuse by Prison and Jail Staff Proves Persistent, Pandemic, PRISON LEGAL NEWS, Feb. 21, 2014, available at https://www.prisonlegalnews.org/

21225_displayArticle.aspx (summarizing many recent cases of sexual assault and rape in prisons across the country).

[25] See Complaint at 3-5, Doe v. Denning, No. 1:08-cv-01265, Doc. 1 (Mar. 3, 2008, N.D. Ill. E. Div.), available at http://ia600402.us.archive.org/31/items/gov.uscourts.ilnd.217697/gov.uscourts.ilnd.217697.1.0.pdf.

[26] See id. at 4.

[27] See Testimony by the Correctional Association of New York Before the Senate Judiciary Committee's Subcommittee on the Constitution, Civil Rights and Human Rights, supra note 32, at 4 ("[I]solation can compromise women's ability to fulfill their particular needs related to reproductive health care, for instance by impeding pregnant women's access to critical obstetrical services, preventing them from getting the regular exercise and movement vital for a healthy pregnancy. Similarly, women in isolation may be dissuaded from requesting care related to sensitive gynecological issues because they are required to inform correction officers about details of their medical problem, may have serious difficulty accessing appropriate medical staff when they do reach out, may be shackled during gynecological appointments that do occur, and will often interact with medical providers in full view of correction officers and/or receive superficial evaluations through closed cell doors."); Interview with Gail Smith, Exec. Dir. CLAIM IL (May 15, 2013).

[28] GLAZE & MARUSCHAK, supra note 17, at 4.

[29] SUSAN D. PHILLIPS, THE SENTENCING PROJECT, VIDEO VISITS FOR CHILDREN WHOSE PARENTS ARE INCARCERATED: IN WHOSE BEST INTERESTS? 1-2 (2012), available at http://sentencingproject.org/doc/publications/cc_Video_Visitation_White_Paper.pdf (describing the importance of and barriers to visitation of incarcerated parents).

[30] Id., at 3-5 (recognizing that video visitation is not a substitute for face-to-face visits, but can be useful when used in addition to face-to-face visits); THE UNIVERSITY OF VERMONT, PRISON VIDEO CONFERENCING 2 (noting in-person visitation is most effective and advising that virtual visitation should be used to increase parent-child contact, not to replace in-person visitation); Graham v. Graham, 794 A.2d 912, 915 (Pa. Super. Ct. 2002) (noting virtual visitation is not equivalent to in-person visitation for a parent).

In: Youth in Solitary Confinement
Editor: Meghan Lloyd
ISBN: 978-1-63483-530-5


*Chapter 3*

# TESTIMONY OF MARC A. LEVIN, DIRECTOR, CENTER FOR EFFECTIVE JUSTICE AT THE TEXAS PUBLIC POLICY FOUNDATION. HEARING ON "REASSESSING SOLITARY CONFINEMENT II: THE HUMAN RIGHTS, FISCAL AND PUBLIC SAFETY CONSEQUENCES"*

## A. INTRODUCTION

The Texas Public Policy Foundation (TPPF) is a conservative think tank. Our mission is to promote and defend liberty, personal responsibility, and free enterprise, and in 2005 the Foundation launched the Center for Effective Justice, which has worked with all three branches of Texas government to advance solutions that emphasize offender and system accountability, empowerment and restoration for victims of crime, and fiscal responsibility. We've assisted with reforms in Texas that have led to the closing of 10 juvenile and adult correctional facilities while at the same time achieving crime reductions that have surpassed the overall national decline. Texas now has its lowest crime rate since 1968.[1] In 2010, the Texas Public Policy

* This is an edited, reformatted and augmented version of testimony presented February 25, 2014 before the Senate Judiciary Committee, Subcommittee on the Constitution, Civil Rights and Human Rights.

Foundation launched Right on Crime, which is a national clearinghouse for conservative criminal justice reforms. The Right On Crime Statement of Principles has been signed by many of the country's most prominent conservative leaders.

As conservatives, we are appropriately skeptical of government that is too large, too intrusive, and too costly, and we insist on accountability and transparency. Government is at its most restrictive when it imposes solitary confinement so it is only appropriate that we bring a critical focus to this issue rather than succumb to an out of sight, out of mind mentality. While we recognize solitary confinement is needed in some instances, policies and practices must be implemented to ensure it is not unnecessarily used to the detriment of public safety, taxpayers, and justice.

The U.S. Bureau of Prisons (BOP) maintained approximately 12,400 inmates in solitary confinement at the time of the May 2013 General Accounting Office (GAO) report, although BOP officials claim the segregated population has declined since then. Many more inmates are so housed in state prisons, which typically means 23 hours alone in a small cell with no stimulation or interaction with other people. The GAO report found that the use of solitary confinement has been growing in the federal prison system despite a lack of any available evidence that this practice was increasing safety for inmates and staff.[2] The GAO report also for the first time revealed the actual cost of solitary confinement on the federal level, finding that it amounts to $78,000 per inmate per year, nearly three times that of housing inmates in the general population.[3] Since the time of the last Senate hearing on solitary confinement, BOP has agreed to begin an audit that will, for the first time, lead to some outside scrutiny of BOP's use of segregation.

The research in this area and the recent successes that several states have achieved in both reducing solitary confinement and improving order in their correctional facilities suggests that there are changes in policies and practices from which both the BOP and state prison systems can benefit.

## B. Solitary Confinement Can Endanger Public Safety

While often viewed primarily as a moral issue, solitary confinement has significant implications for public safety. First and foremost, prisons must discontinue the practice of releasing inmates directly from solitary confinement to the public.

A study in Washington state found that inmates released directly from the Supermax prison, which consists entirely of solitary confinement, committed new felonies at a rate 35 percent greater than that for inmates of the same risk profile released from the general population.[4] Additionally, a greater percentage of the new crimes committed by those released from solitary confinement were among the most serious violent felonies.[5]

Despite this finding, many states continue to release inmates directly from solitary confinement, with more than 1,300 such releases in 2011 in Texas alone.[6] In 2013, a Colorado inmate released directly from solitary confinement murdered the state's director of corrections, Tom Clements. Alarmingly, dating back to 2002, half of those released from Colorado prisons who subsequently committed murder served time in solitary confinement, with some discharged directly to the street. However, as documented below, major changes are underway that are significantly reducing overall solitary confinement in Colorado and those discharged directly from this custody level, with the latter figure falling from 221 in 2004 to 70 in 2013.[7]

The average American may understandably wonder, if an inmate is too dangerous for the general population of a prison, how can they live next to me the next day? While inmates who have served their entire sentence must by law be released, this date is not a mystery to corrections officials. Stepping them down to a lower level of custody at least several months prior to release is not too much to ask.

While it is commonsensical to most people that someone who was subjected to 23 hours a day in a cell with no stimulation will have great difficulty reentering society the next day, the negative effects of solitary confinement on those who were mentally ill even prior to entering solitary confinement are well documented. *The Journal of the American Academy of Psychiatry Law* noted: "The stress, lack of meaningful social contact, and unstructured days can exacerbate symptoms of illness or provoke recurrence. Suicides occur disproportionately more often in segregation units than elsewhere in prison."[8] One study found that 45 percent of prisoners in solitary confinement suffered from serious mental illness, marked psychological symptoms, psychological breakdowns, or brain damage.[9]

## C. Jurisdictions Have Proved Solitary Confinement Can Be Safely Reduced

One of the most stunning examples of downsizing solitary confinement comes from Mississippi. In 2007, Mississippi had 1,300 inmates in solitary confinement while today there are only 300.[10] This downsizing has saved Mississippi taxpayers $6 million, because solitary confinement costs $102 per day compared to $42 a day for inmates in the general population.[11] Most importantly, violence within Mississippi's prisons and the recidivism rate upon release are both down, with violence dropping nearly 70 percent.[12]

Maine is a similar success story. In 2011, the state prison in Warren instituted a plan to reduce long-term segregation which has resulted in a decline in the segregated population from 139 in August 2011 to between 35 and 45 inmates just a year later.[13] Importantly, Maine Corrections Commissioner Joseph Ponte said the downsizing of solitary confinement has led to "substantial reductions in violence, reductions in use of force, reductions in use of chemicals, reductions in use of restraint chairs, reductions in inmates cutting [themselves] up — which was an event that happened every week or at least every other week...The cutting has] almost been totally eliminated as a result of these changes."[14]

Some of the changes involved reducing the duration of solitary confinement – for example, those segregated for drugs can now graduate out of confinement and stay in the general population as long as they pass drug tests. Moreover, there was a change in the chain of command. Rather than the shift captain being able to place an inmate in segregation for more than three days, the segregation unit manager and the housing unit manager must agree after this period to continue the segregation and that decision must be ratified by the Commissioner.

Similarly, in the last decade, Ohio dramatically reduced its solitary confinement population from 800 to 90 prisoners.[15] Additionally, from September 2011 to September 2013, Colorado cut the number of inmates in solitary confinement from 1,505 to 662. The number of mentally ill offenders in solitary confinement has fallen even more sharply and Colorado Department of Corrections Executive Director Rick Raemisch has proposed that, for those mentally ill offenders who are not redirected to a secure treatment program, they be given at least 20 hours of out-of-cell programming per week.

It is important to note that prison staff do not necessarily want more inmates to be in solitary confinement. In fact, in January 2014, the association representing Texas prison guards, AFSCME Texas Correctional Employees Local 3807, called for reducing the solitary confinement of death row inmates, noting that because "inmates have very few privileges to lose," staff become easy targets.[16]

There have been some incremental advances in improving Texas' use of solitary confinement. In 2013, a provision was enacted requiring an independent study of solitary confinement that is now getting underway. Also, bills that were proposed on this issue in the last several legislative sessions brought the matter to the attention of corrections leaders. At hearings on the legislation, Texas Department of Criminal Justice (TDCJ) officials were called to testify to explain their policies and practices and it was apparent that, while legislators did not want to micromanage the agency, they wanted to see progress. From 2007 to the most recent report, the number of inmates in solitary confinement in Texas prisons, referred to as administrative segregation, has dropped from 9,347 to 8,238.[17] These figures do not include those in "safekeeping," a form of protective custody for vulnerable inmates such as former police officers.

One of the keys to the modest reduction in solitary confinement in Texas has been the elimination of the waiting list for the Gang Renunciation and Disassociation Program (GRAD) where inmates can earn their way out of solitary confinement by renouncing their gang affiliation and receive protection during the process. Notably, none of the inmates who have completed this program have ever returned to solitary confinement.[18] In Texas, unlike many other states, inmates can be placed in solitary confinement not only for disciplinary violations, but also upon initial entry into prison if they are suspected to be gang members. This is why the GRAD program is particularly important.

More broadly, any intervention that reduces prison violence is likely to reduce solitary confinement by avoiding the incidents that often lead to it. One of the best models for promoting order in prisons is the parallel universe model embraced by Arizona in 2004 through the "Getting Ready" program, which won the innovation award from the Harvard University JFK School of Government. The parallel universe model attempts to make prison more like ordinary life in that how the inmate is treated is directly related to their behavior. For example, inmates who are exemplary, both in completing educational and treatment programs, holding a job inside of prison, and maintaining an unblemished disciplinary record, have a longer curfew and receive better food. Since the program was implemented, inmate violence has decreased by 37 percent, inmate-on-staff assaults by 51 percent, and inmate suicides by 33 percent.[19] So many inmates are working through the program that they have contributed more than $1 million to a fund for victims of crime, and recidivism rates of participants are 35 percent lower than for similar inmates.[20]

By the same token, the swift and certain sanctions model that is so successful in the HOPE Court certainly has a place inside prisons. It is a bit more challenging to apply a matrix of intermediate sanctions in prison because there are fewer privileges that inmates have that can constitutionally be withheld, as compared with those on probation or parole. However, such sanctions can include withholding access to the commissary, withholding access to the phone and mail except to communicate with an attorney, relocation to a less desirable cell or higher security unit and away from any inmate with whom they have a dispute, and even short stints in solitary confinement of 24 to 72 hours. Required anger management programming should also be available as a response to misconduct. While inmates who instigate force causing serious bodily harm to a staff member or other inmate should be placed in solitary confinement for a significant period of time rather than dealt with through intermediate sanctions, these intermediate sanctions can address the more common, less severe disciplinary infractions before they escalate to that point.

However, perhaps the most effective sanction is sometimes not available due to policies that result in a large share of inmates serving all or nearly all of their sentence behind bars, regardless of their behavior. Those inmates eligible for parole typically realize that their record of behavior inside prison will be a major factor in whether they will be approved for parole. In those states with good time or earned time policies, the only way an inmate can earn time off their sentence is through good behavior, though under earned time policies they often must go beyond that by completing treatment, educational, and vocational programs. Yet, the federal government and many states abolished parole in the 1990's, even for nonviolent offenders. Some of these same states such as Florida also adopted so-called truth-in-sentencing policies that require even nonviolent offenders to serve 85 to 90 percent of their sentences beyond bars.

However, a 2013 a study conducted by the Pew Charitable States Public Safety Performance Project of New Jersey of inmates released from prison found that comparable inmates placed on parole supervision committed 36 percent fewer new offenses, casting doubt on policies such as the abolishment of parole that have led to more inmates maxing out their entire term behind bars.[21] Not only does the elimination of parole and requirements that inmates serve virtually all their time in prison put prison growth on auto-pilot, these policies create another drawback that is relevant here. That is, many inmates know that, unless they go so far as to commit another crime in prison, they will be released on the same date or virtually the same date regardless of their behavior. The same drawback applies to life without parole sentences, which while justified in many of the cases in which they are imposed due to the heinousness of the crime and a pattern of violence, are being served by inmates in Louisiana for offenses such as marijuana and stealing a belt.[22] While Louisiana is the state with the most nonviolent offenders serving life without parole, the federal system dwarfs all states, accounting for two-thirds of the 3,278 prisoners serving life without parole in 2013 for nonviolent offenses. By reducing the share of inmates, particularly nonviolent inmates, who must serve all or virtually all of their entire terms behind bars, we can ensure that more inmates have an incentive to avoid the types of misconduct that often lead to solitary confinement.

## D. Recommendations

The successful experiences of several states and the empirical research in this area lead to many recommendations that can reduce the unnecessary use of solitary confinement while promoting order in correctional facilities. These include:

1) End the practice of releasing inmates directly from solitary confinement.
2) Ensure that there is an oversight mechanism, whether that is an ombudsman or the head of the department, to review decisions to keep an inmate in solitary confinement beyond 72 hours. This is particularly important in states like Texas where inmates can be placed in solitary confinement simply for being a suspected gang member, a determination which is prone to human error.
3) Provide a means for inmates to earn their way out of solitary confinement, such as through a period of exemplary behavior and gang renunciation, if they were not placed there for instigating force that caused serious bodily injury to a staff member or other inmate.
4) Eliminate rules that make all inmates in solitary confinement ineligible for any programing and allow such inmates access to constructive reading materials, including educational course books.

5) Enhance training for prison personnel in de-escalation techniques, mental illness, and mental retardation, issues which often lead to solitary confinement. Some states such as Nebraska are looking at having some higher level prison guard positions filled by individuals with degrees in areas such as social work who are better equipped to not just respond to behavior, but change it.
6) Require agencies to include in their annual or biennial budget proposals an estimate of the additional cost attributable to solitary confinement.
7) Implement a parallel universe model that creates incentives for positive behavior and self-improvement.
8) Create a matrix of intermediate sanctions that must be used prior to placing an inmate in solitary confinement for more than 72 hours, unless that inmate has instigated force that caused serious bodily injury to a staff member or other inmate.
9) For nonviolent inmates, restore parole and allow for earned time, thereby reducing the number of "dead-enders" and allowing for substantial variation in time served based on the inmate's performance. We recommend the pending bills before this Committee by Senators Whitehouse and Portman (S. 1675) and Cornyn (S. 1783) that would expand earned time for nonviolent offenders.
10) Enact into law the Smarter Sentencing Act (S. 1410), introduced by Chairman Durbin and Senator Lee, and cosponsored by Ranking Member Cruz, which will reduce overcrowding in the federal system so that we can focus on the most serious offenders, lead to safer institutions, and save billions that can also be used for other important public safety priorities. Overcrowding can contribute to the overuse of solitary confinement by leading to an insufficient number of guards to control inmates in the general population and making it more difficult to separate inmates and groups of inmates who may have issues with one another.
11) Utilize "missioned housing," which are separate, smaller correctional settings, for inmates in segregation as protective custody, such as former police officers and those who have recently exited a gang, as well as for mentally ill and developmentally delayed inmates who were segregated due to an inability to follow orders. These inmates who did not harm another inmate or staff member should not be subject to 23 hours of solitary confinement alongside those who committed acts of violence behind bars. The Wisconsin model of

Special Management Units provides an example of such "missioned housing" for these types of inmates.

12) Reexamine prison construction and renovation plans, including the planned BOP retrofitting of the Thomson unit purchased from Illinois, to ensure unnecessary Supermax/solitary confinement beds are not added. Even if additional maximum security capacity is needed, the vast majority or all of the beds can be general population beds.
13) Other states should join the BOP and states such as Illinois and Maryland in bringing in an outside organization, such as the Vera Institute, to provide a perspective from outside the system, analyze data, and help train wardens and other personnel in alternative strategies. Vera provided technical support to Washington and Ohio in successfully reducing solitary confinement and is now working with Illinois and Maryland through their Segregation Reduction Project to analyze data, and help train wardens and other personnel in alternative strategies. In Illinois, for example, Vera found that 85% of the more than 2,000 inmates in solitary confinement were placed there for less severe types of infractions and that the average length of stay was some 2.8 years.[23]
14) Improve availability of data. For example, there is no reliable data on the number of inmates in different types of segregation (punitive versus protective) and very little data at all on local jails and immigration detention centers.

## E. Conclusion

It is doubtful that any prison warden ever lost their job for putting an inmate in solitary confinement. Prison officials are rightly worried about being held to account for prison violence and escapes. Consequently, absent independent scrutiny and a focus on this issue at the highest level in a corrections agency, the natural incentive within the system can be to use solitary confinement excessively. As conservatives who believe in holding institutions accountable, we must be especially vigilant in shining a light into these darkest recesses of government. Now, that light is illuminating policies and practices that can lead to greater public safety through improved offender outcomes, lower costs to taxpayers, and more orderly correctional facilities.

## End Notes

[1] Marc Levin and Jeanette Moll, "Texas Is Still Tough on Crime, But Now More Effective," Texas Public Policy Foundation, March 2013, http://www.texaspolicy.com/sites/default/files/docufflments/2013-03-PB06- TexasToughonCrime-CEJ-MarcLevinJeanetteMoll.pdf.

[2] "Improvements Needed in Bureau of Prisons' Monitoring and Evaluation of Impact of Segregated Housing, General Accounting Office, May 2013, http://www.gao.gov/assets/660/654349.pdf.

[3] Ibid.

[4] David Lowell, et. al., "Recidivism of Supermax Prisoners in Washington State," Crime & Delinquency, Oct.2007, vol. 53 no. 4 633-656, http://cad.sagepub.com/content/53/4/633.abstract.

[5] Ibid.

[6] Testimony of Travis Leete, Texas Criminal Justice Coalition, April 17, 2013, http://www.texascjc.org/sites/default/files/uploads/HB%201266%20Testimony%20(Ad%20Seg%20Review).pdf.

[7] Jennifer Brown and Karen Krummy, "Half of parolees who murdered spent time in solitary confinement," Denver Post, Sept. 23, 2013, http://www.denverpost.com/ parole/ci_ 24140370/half-parolees-who-murderedspent-time-solitary-confinement. Rick Raemish, "My Night in Solitary," New York Times, Feb. 20, 2014, http://www.nytimes. com/2014/02/21/opinion/my-night-in-solitary.html?_r=0.

[8] Jeffrey L. Metzner, MD and Jamie Fellner Esq., "Solitary Confinement and Mental Illness in U.S. Prisons: A Challengefor Medical Ethics," J Am Acad Psychiatry Law 38:1:104-108 (March 2010), http://www.jaapl.org/content/38/1/104.full.

[9] D. Lovell, Patterns of disturbed behavior in a supermax population, Criminal Justice and Behavior, 35, 985-1004 (2008).

[10] Randall Pinkston, "Mississippi Rethinks Solitary Confinement," CBS News, May 18, 2013, http://www.cbsnews.com/news/mississippi-rethinks-solitary-confinement/.

[11] Ibid.

[12] Terry Kupers et al., "Beyond Supermax Administrative Segregation: Mississippi's Experience Rethinking Prison Classification and Creating Alternative Mental Health Programs," Criminal Justice and Behavior 36 (2009): 1037- 50, https://www.aclu.org/files/images asset_upload_file359_41136.pdf.

[13] Alex Barber, "Less restriction equals less violence at Maine State Prison," Bangor Daily News, June 15, 2012, http://bangordailynews.com/2012/06/15/news/state/less-restriction-equals-less-violence-at-maine-state-prison/.

[14] Ibid.

[15] Terry Kupers et al., "Beyond Supermax Administrative Segregation: Mississippi's Experience Rethinking Prison Classification and Creating Alternative Mental Health Programs," Criminal Justice and Behavior 36 (2009): 1037- 50, https://www.aclu.org/files/images/asset_upload_file359_41136.pdf.

[16] Nicholas Flatow, "Texas Prison Guards Vie For Less Solitary Confinement." Think Progress, Jan. 30, 2014, http://thinkprogress.org/justice/2014/01/30/3223731/texas-prison-guards-vie-solitary-confinement/#.

[17] TDCJ Statistical Reports for 2007 and 2012, http://www.tdcj.state.tx.us/documents/Statistical_Report_FY2007.pdf
http://www.tdcj.state.tx.us/documents/Statistical_Report_FY2012.pdf.

[18] "Leaving Gang Life Behind in Texas," Correcitons.com, http://www.corrections.com/articles/3071.

[19] Ann Coppola, "A Parallel Universe," Correcitons.com, http://www.corrections.com/news/article/20339.

[20] Ibid.

[21] The Pew Charitable Trusts, "The Impact of Parole in New Jersey," November 2013. Available at: http://www.pewstates.org/uploadedFiles/PCS_Assets/2013/PSPP_NJParole-Brief.pdf

[22] "A Living Death: Life Without Parole for Nonviolent Offenses," American Civil Liberties Union, November 2013, https://www.aclu.org/files/assets/111213a-lwop-complete-report.pdf.

[23] Testimony of Michael Jacobson, Director of the Vera Institute, June 19, 2012, http://www.vera.org/files/michael-jacobson-testimony-on-solitary-confinement-2012.pdf.

In: Youth in Solitary Confinement
Editor: Meghan Lloyd
ISBN: 978-1-63483-530-5


*Chapter 4*

# TESTIMONY OF DAMON THIBODEAUX. HEARING ON "REASSESSING SOLITARY CONFINEMENT II: THE HUMAN RIGHTS, FISCAL AND PUBLIC SAFETY CONSEQUENCES"*

Chairman Durbin, Ranking Member Cruz, and members of the Subcommittee, thank you for inviting me to testify today. My name is Damon Thibodeaux. When I was 22 years old, I was arrested, interrogated by police, and coerced into falsely confessing to raping and murdering my 14-year-old cousin. In October 1997, I was tried and convicted for capital murder and sentenced to death. I was then sent to the Louisiana State Penitentiary at Angola where I spent a month shy of 15 years in solitary confinement before I was exonerated and released in late September 2012. I then became the 141st known actually innocent death-row exoneree since the Supreme Court reinstated capital punishment in 1976. I was the 18th death row inmate since that time to be exonerated based at least in part on DNA evidence.

I do not really have the words to tell you fully how much physical, mental, and emotional harm is done to those of us who are placed into solitary confinement for any length of time, but I want to thank you for this chance to give you at least some idea about what we are doing to people when we confine them in this way.

* This is an edited, reformatted and augmented version of testimony presented February 25, 2014 before the Senate Judiciary Committee, Subcommittee on the Constitution, Civil Rights and Human Rights.

I spent my years at Angola, while my lawyers fought to prove my innocence, in a cell that measured about 8 feet by 10 feet. It had three solid walls all painted white, a cell door, a sink, a toilet, a desk and seat attached to a wall, and an iron bunk with a thin mattress. These four walls are your life. Being in that environment for 23 hours a day will slowly kill you. Mentally, you have to find some way to live as if you were not there. If you cannot do that, you will die a slow mental death and may actually wish for your physical death, so that you do not have to continue that existence. More than anything, solitary confinement is an existence without hope.

Fairly early during my confinement at Angola, I very seriously considered giving up my legal rights and letting the State execute me. I was at the point where I did not want to live like an animal in a cage for years on end, only to lose my case and then have the State kill me anyway. I thought it would be better to end my life as soon as I could and avoid the agony of life in solitary. Fortunately, my lawyer and friend, Denise LeBoeuf, convinced me that I would be exonerated and released someday, and she gave me hope to keep fighting and living.

The food, such as it was, was brought to us whenever the prison decided it was time to feed us. It consisted often of nothing more than rice and gravy, and sometimes rotten vegetables that could not be sold in stores to people on the outside. The diet was high in salt, carbohydrates, and fat, and, together with the lack of normal activity and exercise, caused many of the men to develop diabetes, heart disease, and other serious ailments. I estimate that about 70 percent of the inmates on death row at Angola had heart and dental issues, largely from the food and other conditions. Inmates would go untreated because they could not afford treatment. One inmate could not walk after years of solitary confinement. I developed high blood pressure and high cholesterol, problems that disappeared after my release and return to a decent diet and normal activity.

The heat inside death row was unbearable during the long summers in Louisiana because we were denied air-conditioning. The prison actually blew hot air from the outside into the death row building, raising temperatures into the 100-130 degree range in each cell and making our existence there all the more unbearable. We would sit in our cells with the sweat dripping down our bodies. Some would strip and lie on the floor where they would also try to sleep. But, if we had to leave the cell or if a tour group came through to stare at us, we had to dress in our jumpsuits, no matter how hot it was. Those who had heart disease or diabetes suffered the most.

In the winter, the problem was exactly the opposite. The temperatures in the cells were often in the 40-50 degree range because we often did not have heat. We collected sweatshirts and blankets to stay warm. Some of the men could not afford them, so we would give them our sweatshirts to stay warm. But, if someone could not help you, you just sat there and shivered. We treat pets and animals better than this. If you treated animals this way, you would get arrested and prosecuted, but that is apparently not the case with humans.

People would come to death row to tour our cells as if we were in a zoo. I sometimes thought that they brought tour groups from schools and churches into death row just to see how difficult it was for us there. We are, as the prison tells these visitors, the "worst of the worst" and do not deserve to be treated humanely.

Inmates in solitary have no job and no educational or job training opportunities. The time passes painfully and slowly.

In solitary confinement, we spent our time waiting for exoneration, execution, or the reduction of our death sentences to life in prison. We have access to television on a shared basis with another inmate, and the viewing is limited to whatever the prison permits. We can read books if someone on the outside can afford to buy them for us from Amazon or some other approved seller, or if inmates share the books they have received. I understand that some inmates in some prisons do not have these same privileges and they must come up with other ways to keep their minds from slipping.

No one, no matter how horrible the crimes for which they have been convicted, can endure this lack of stimulation, contact, and activity for very long. I saw men lose their minds. Some screamed at all hours of the night. Some just stared at a wall, even when they could spend their one hour a day outside of the cell. Some were drugged to the point that they seemed nearly comatose. Some tried to save their medications and overdose on them to commit suicide. I saw men smear their feces in their cells. For 15 years, I watched the State slowly execute many of my fellow inmates before it could legally put the needle into their arms.

To make the time pass as best that I could, I exercised in my cell two or three times a day. During the one hour each day that I was out of my cell, I could shower, call my lawyer, or take care of whatever else I needed to do. On three days each week, I could spend that one hour outdoors in what was basically a caged dog-run. Depending on the weather, I might stay inside and exercise in the hallway by running back and forth. I did not see the night sky or stars during those 15 years. Sleep was often a problem because I was so inactive and mentally dulled during the day.

To keep my mind occupied as best that I was able, I watched the news, listened to the radio or cds, and read what I could. I repeated this same routine over and over again, day after day, for 15 years. The monotony was interrupted only by a visit or phone call with one of my lawyers or, rarely, a visit from a family member. These visits, which not everyone gets, occurred about once every five years. I would not permit my son, who was five years old when I was incarcerated at Angola, to visit and see me in that condition. I insisted that he wait until I was exonerated before we met. Only on the day of my release on September 28, 2012, when he was 20 years old, did I see him for the first time since my arrest in July 1996. I believed that seeing me in those conditions at Angola would be harmful to both of us.

Since my release, I have seen a psychologist who has helped me understand how I have to view my time in solitary for a crime that I did not commit and how to keep it from causing me even more harm. I have suffered a number of long-term effects from solitary confinement, including difficulty engaging and speaking with people on some occasions.

I do not condone what those who have killed and committed other serious offenses have done. But, I also do not condone what we do to them when we put them in solitary for years on end and treat them as less than human. We are better than that or, at least, we like to think that we are. Why do we think it is necessary to do this to anyone and what benefit are we gaining by doing it? It's torture, pure and simple, no matter what else we want to call it. Very few people in this country have any idea that we are keeping thousands of people in solitary confinement and what we are doing to them by doing that.

I thank the Subcommittee for looking at this situation and educating the public about it.

# INDEX

## C



## D

## I



## J



## K



## L

## M



## N



## O



## P

## Q



## R



## S

## T



## U

## V



## W



## Y